The Royal Navy at PORTLAND Since 1845

Geoffrey Carter

MARITIME BOOKS
1987

Dedicated to the memory of

CAPTAIN ANTHONY NIGEL WIGLEY RN,
of HMS OSPREY, Portland,

killed on the afternoon of Monday, 3 December 1984,
when his Wessex V helicopter crashed onto the
breakwater of Portland harbour.

Acknowledgements

In addition to those mentioned in the introduction, I would like to acknowledge with gratitude the response of the following to my requests for information on aspects of this history:

C.G. Ashover, Mrs M. Attwooll, R. Bishop, F.W.P. Bourne, A.E. Bristow, D. Cobb, R.M.C. Corbett, Capt. C.J.S. Craig DSC RN (HMS Osprey), N. Dimon, Dr T. Dinsdale, S. Dobson, D. Dwyer the "Foylebank" Association: Fleet Air Arm Museum, A. Gibson, J. Hinton, G. Hudson, J. Laing, J Makin OBE, J. Russell Smith, Lt. Cdr. R.A. Safe RN (Fleet Photographic Officer), A. Scott, CPO Tierney and the staff of the Photographic Section HMS Osprey, G.S. Timothy, R. Van Riel, W.J. Ward, M.E. Walker, Lt. Cdr. J. Wallace RN (Retd), Instr. Lt. Cdr G. Wanklin RN(Retd), F. White.

Geoffrey Carter

CONTENTS

Portland Naval Base 1987—A birds eye view.

INTRODUCTION

I first came to Weymouth as a small boy in the 1930s, staying with relatives, and it was then that my interest in the Royal Navy began. On one occasion I visited the battleship HMS *Malaya* at anchor in Weymouth Bay, and had tea with my uncle who was serving aboard her. On another occasion I was taken round the dockyard by a family friend and remember particularly the floating dock and the railway lines! However, it was not until I came to live and work in Dorset in 1968 that I began to collect information on the naval side of the history of Portland. Until recently the preparation of the work has been very much a part time and occasional activity, but more time over the past two years has enabled me at last to complete the narrative.

This study does not concern itself with naval activity at Portland before the man-made harbour of refuge was begun after the Royal Commission of 1845. It is known that for centuries men o' war anchored in the lee of the isle of Portland to shelter from the prevailing south westerly winds. Ships sailed from Weymouth Bay to attack and harrass the Spanish Armada in 1588, and a battle with the Dutch Admiral Van Tromp was fought off Portland by Admiral Blake in 1653. After an eighteenth century expedition to sack the town of Cherbourg in 1758 the English fleet returned to Portland Roads, and actions were fought against French privateers. When King George III came to Weymouth in the late eighteenth century he reviewed such naval vessels as were anchored in the Roads and is known to have taken short cruises in the *Southampton* (32 guns) and *Magnificent* (74 guns). But from 1845 onwards the relationship between Portland, Weymouth and the Royal Navy drew ever closer with the establishment of a naval base at Portland. It is the work of this base and the ships and men serving there that forms the subject of this story. In very general terms Portland is taken to include the sea area of the English Channel between a line drawn south from St Alban's or St Aldhelm's Head in the east to Start Point in the west.

A large part of the story is taken up with the period 1939-45. From 1940, until the end of the European war, Portland was literally in the front line. Not only that, but as a salient, it jutted out into the English Channel towards the enemy coast. In both defence and offence, it played a full and at times dramatic part on the naval side of war in the 'narrow sea'.

Many people have helped me in providing the material for this work. Commander C W Eason RN, the Queen's Harbourmaster at Portland, first gave of his time to talk to me about the history of the base, advised me on local sources and allowed me to walk most of the length of the breakwaters. Some ten years later, Captain A Wigley RN gave particular support before his untimely death.

A host of others, past and present officers and men of the Royal Navy, members of the WRNS, and civilians engaged in the work of the base or the research establishments on Portland, have given of their time in interview and correspondence. The main sources of evidence, however, are drawn from documentary and photographic archives. The staff of the Public Records Office, the Imperial War Museum, the National Maritime Museum, the Dorset County Museum, the Dorset County Records Office and the Weymouth Reference Library have all proved once again their value and support to researchers.

Finally, the work could never have been completed without the support of my wife and family. They have endured the conversations, the writing, the piles of papers and photographs and books, the typing and retyping, and not demurred at the expense of frequent visits, particularly to London, as part of the research.

1

THE HARBOUR OF REFUGE

Eighteenth century mariners sailing eastwards along the northern shore of the English Channel were warned of the dangers present as they sought to pass the island of Portland, particularly at night. The great curve of West Bay swept round from due east opposite Bridport to west of south at Portland Bill. Two lights, north and south of each other, shone from positions close to the Bill. The warnings were quite specific:

On first sight of these lights, if you are in or near the bay, be sure to haul off to the southward; and when you have brought the lights in line, you will then be passing the race and so proceeding East by South will avoid the Shambles. But, if you cannot sail south of the race, then if the winds be strong south westerly, you may safely sail between the race and the bill, especially at a slack or ebb tide. When you have sailed north east about a league, you may turn into Portland Road, where is a very strong anchoring and eight or nine fathoms of water. If neither of the above mentioned can be done, then it is to be observed that (close to the shore) the current during the flood sets so strong that if you can but get into it you cannot come ashore if you would. Insomuch as it will give you an opportunity for sailing between the Bill and the Race as above directed, or else (though with much difficulty in avoiding the Race) carry you to the South thereof.

But if you should happen to be deep imbayed, as that neither anchoring, nor the foregoing directions can be practised, then it is to be noted that between Burton and Chesil, there is a steep beach of pebbles near which it ebbs nine hours and flows three and if you can especially at the beginning of the ebb, run your ship boldly on the said beach, and then remain on board for five or six seas, you may step ashore with greater safety, but if you leave the ship instantly, it is certainly fatal.

The number of ships lost in West Bay was a testament to the dangers west of Portland in the prevailing winds. The Roads to the east offered protection from these winds, but even then, in the less frequent easterlies, the seas could become most unpleasant.

By the turn of the eighteenth century there were proposals to build a breakwater jutting out into Portland Roads and Weymouth Bay. It was clear from the start that there were two major considerations in establishing a protected anchorage. Firstly, there was no such facility on the English side of the Channel between Devonport and the ports adjacent to the Solent. Secondly, there were the needs of national defence. France, the 'old enemy', was developing the port of Cherbourg as a naval base and it was inevitable that a counter move should be made in England. Portland was well placed to the north-north-west of the French port.

As early as 1795, John Harvey, postmaster at Weymouth, had put forward the idea of a breakwater. In 1827 he published a pamphlet entitled "Remarks on Portland Breakwater", in which he reviewed the development and strategic effects of the great fortified harbour being built at Cherbourg, only 21 leagues from Portland. He then proposed that a breakwater should be built extending from Portland north east for two and a half miles, terminating at the wreck of the *Earl of Abergavenny*. This ship had struck the Shambles bank, had then headed for the shore in Weymouth Bay, and sank two and a half miles off the beach on 5 February 1805. The long sea wall proposed by Harvey would not only create a sheltered anchorage, but would also protect the harbour, pier and bathing places of Weymouth from the south east winds. It was estimated that the breakwater would take five years to build using stone readily available in large quantities on Portland itself. The stone could be brought to sea level by means of an inclined railway.

The decision actually to build a breakwater was the result of the Commission of Enquiry into Harbours of Refuge set up in 1844. In June of that year HMS *Fearless* surveyed the waters enclosed by Portland and Weymouth Bay. The responsibility of the Commissioners extended beyond Portland, and in their report presented to the House of Commons in 1845, they considered also the claims of Dover and Seaford.

The commissioners began to take evidence about Portland on Tuesday 28 May 1844 with Admiral Sir Thomas Byam Martin in the chair. The first witness was Lieutenant William Marshall RN who commanded the revenue cruiser *Adelaide* and who had served on the Portland station for seven years. He was asked:

> Do you think that if there were a breakwater vessels would go into West Bay in an easterly wind, or prefer the protection of a breakwater?

Marshall replied that in his opinion they would prefer the breakwater, for there ships would be safe if the wind changed suddenly to the southward, whereas if sheltering in West Bay they would get imbayed with a great risk of disaster. He was questioned on the desirability of an opening between the breakwater and the shore. He favoured an opening for small vessels but not for large ones because baffling winds close to high land could create sailing difficulties. He was more agreeable to a suggestion that there might be an opening in the middle of the breakwater. Towards the end of the examination of Lieutenant Marshall, Admiral Dundas, another member of the Commission, asked a question he put to most of the other witnesses:

> In time of war, in the present state of Portland and Weymouth Roads, could a fleet of men of war and armed steamers rendezvous there in all winds and weathers, or would it be beneficial to the objects I have stated to have a breakwater made in Portland Roads?

Lieutenant Marshall replied:

> I think that, as at present they would run a risk, a breakwater would ensure this object at all times.

Mr Lowe, Chief Mate and Commander of the revenue cutter *Petrel*, in his evidence, answered in a similar manner to Lieutenant Marshall. Mr Joseph Read, who had been in the merchant service for thirty years, mostly in the Irish trade, was familiar with Portland waters and recalled that vessels beating down the Channel as far as the Lizard and Start Point were sometimes obliged to try back for the Downs. He had seen as many as sixty to seventy vessels in Portland Roads during south westerly gales. He favoured no opening at all in the breakwater but agreed that men-of-war could keep station and get out of harbour at all times if a breakwater were constructed.

The next day the Commissioners examined Mr Robert White who was employed in the Packet Service. In common with other witnesses he confirmed that there was good holding ground in Portland Roads. During the Napoleonic Wars he had seen as many as one hundred to one hundred and forty vessels in the Roads at one time. He had also been out on surveys into the possibility of building a breakwater as early as 1822 and 1836. With some reservations he approved of an opening in the middle of the breakwater.

Mr Allen, a ship owner resident in Portland, agreed with the advantages offered by a breakwater but disapproved of any opening in it. He believed that the tides would set round the opening and would let in such a sea that the harbour would be less safe than if there were no opening at all. Captain C A Manning, Vice Lieutenant of Portland, a magistrate, and Deputy Lieutenant of Dorset, also gave evidence to the Commission. He was questioned on his experience of ships using Portland Roads in difficult conditions, the extent of Crown property on the island, the availability of stone and the supply of water. Mr Thomas Litt Harvey, son of the John Harvey who had earlier published plans of the breakwater, outlined the scheme his father had put forward, but thought it would now cost £600,000 and take six or seven years to build. He was not in favour of

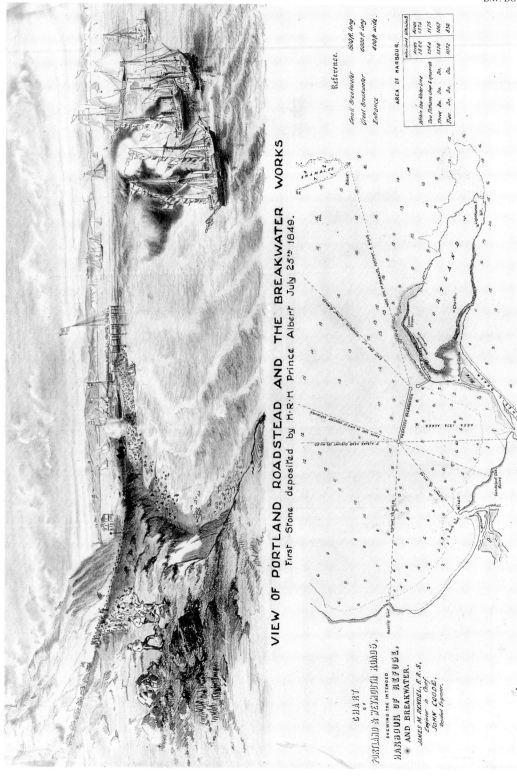

CHART
OF
PORTLAND & WEYMOUTH ROADS,
SHEWING THE INTENDED
HARBOUR OF REFUGE,
AND BREAKWATER.

JAMES M. RENDEL, F.R.S.,
Engineer in Chief,
JOHN COODE,
Resident Engineer.

VIEW OF PORTLAND ROADSTEAD AND THE BREAKWATER WORKS
First Stone deposited by H·R·H Prince Albert July 25th 1849.

Reference.

Small Breakwater	1500 ft. long
Great Breakwater	6000 ft. long
Entrance	400 ft. wide.

AREA OF HARBOUR.

	Acres	Within Given's Breakwater Acres
Within low Water Line	1322	1378
Two Fathoms Low & upwards	1344	1175
Three Do. Do. Do.	1374	1667
Five Do. Do. Do.	1072	832

The ceremony of laying the first stone of the harbour of refuge, 25 July 1849.

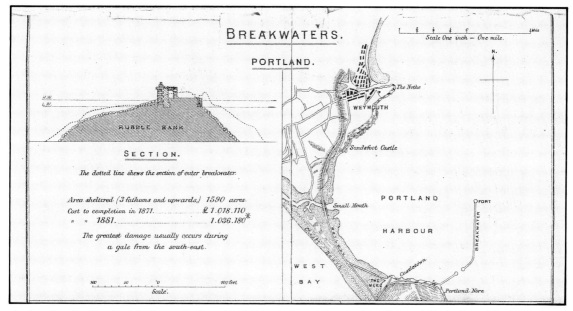

A plan showing Portland harbour of refuge in 1885, together with a section of the rubble bank and harbour wall.

any opening in the wall. The last two witnesses were Mr John Ferrard, harbour master at Weymouth, and Captain Charles Payne RN, a resident, who recalled vessels being driven onto the north shore at Osmington in the south east to south gale in 1824 and considered there was a risk of ships being driven onto a breakwater if it were built.

The conclusion of the Commission was that:

> A squadron, stationed at Portland will have under its protection, jointly with Dartmouth, all the intervening coast, and these places, with Plymouth, will complete the chain of communications and co-operation between Dover and Falmouth, a distance of 300 miles.
>
> There is everything at Portland to render the construction of a breakwater easy, cheap and expeditious, and the holding ground of the Roads is particularly good. A large part of the island facing the Bay is Crown property and contains abundance of stone. It has numerous springs and plenty of the best water may be had in any direction for the supply of ships.
>
> The roadstead also possesses the advantage of an inner harbour at Weymouth.

Three harbours of refuge were proposed. Dover was given first priority, then Portland and finally Seaford. The estimated cost of the harbour of refuge at Portland was given as £500,000. It would be constructed in Portland Bay, would extend a mile and a quarter in a north easterly direction from near the north part of the island and in about seven fathoms of water. It would have an opening of 150 feet a quarter of a mile from the shore. An area of 1200 acres would be sheltered by the construction.

The Portland Harbour and Breakwater Bill was introduced into Parliament and received the Royal Assent on 11 May 1847. Work began on 1 August 1847 under the supervision of Mr J M Rendel as Chief Engineer.

James Meadows Rendel was born near Okehampton in 1799. He was one of the leading engineers of his time and was regarded as energetic, tactful and honest. He was a surveyor under Thomas Telford before moving to Plymouth. From there he engineered roads in North Devon and, in 1824, built the iron bridge over the Catwater at the estuary of the River Plym. He was responsible for the design of the Millbay docks as well as harbour improvements at Newhaven and Littlehampton. He moved to London in 1838. Although the harbour of refuge at Portland was one of his major achievements, he also engineered dock works at Birkenhead, Grimsby, Holyhead and St Peter Port in Guernsey before he died in 1856. After his death his work at Portland was taken over by Mr J Coode, the resident engineer.

Much of the labour for the works was provided by convicts from the new prison at Portland, built for that very purpose. The prison was to hold 1300 prisoners:-

> . . . who will undergo a period of probationary discipline and be employed in the construction of the breakwater prior to their removal to the Australian colonies.

The prisoners were transferred from such establishments as Pentonville and Wakefield, often arrived by ship from Portsmouth, and went through a period of solitary confinement in the cells before joining the working gangs. For some twenty years, convict ships sailed from Portland to Van Diemens Land or Western Australia on voyages that lasted between 75 and 115 days.

The stone used for the breakwater was that inferior material that had to be quarried in order to reach the deeper layers of best quality stone. The buildings at Whitehall and St Pauls Cathedral in London had been built of this fine material and vast piles of inferior stone encumbered the quarries situated on the summit of the island, some 200-300 feet above sea level. The stone was moved by several inclined railways from the quarries to the point where the breakwater joined the shore. The wagons carrying the stone were raised and lowered by wire ropes attached to drums which caused the descending loaded train to draw up the empty one from below. Before the descent, each wagon passed over a weighbridge which measured precisely the quantity of stone being lowered. It was hoped that some 2,000-3,000 tons of stone would be sent down each day when operations were in full swing.

On Wednesday 25 July 1849 the Prince Consort laid the foundation stone of the breakwater. He was received by local dig-
nitaries when he arrived at Dorchester by train. He reached Weymouth earlier than expected and before the Mayor and his party were assembled at the quayside. To make matters worse, the steamer due to take the Mayor and his party to Portland broke down and the navy had to come to their rescue. Members of the public travelled to the opening ceremony in fishing smacks. Prince Albert sailed in the royal yacht *Victoria and Albert*, passing the war steamers *Stromboli*, *Nautilus*, *Sphynx*, *Myrtle* and *Fanny*, anchored off the island. At the stone-laying ceremony, Mr Coode, the Resident Engineer, presented a copper container to Prince Albert. Various coins were placed inside it before the container itself was sealed within the stone. Apart from laying the stone, the Prince also visited the prison, presenting a Bible and Prayer Book to the Chapel, in which he wrote:-

> Presented to the chapel of the convicts of Portland, in token of interest, and in hope of their amendment.
>
> Albert

He continued to show his interest in the harbour works and visited both the breakwater and the prison before his death.

By 1859, Mr Coode, then Engineer in Chief, could see:-

> hundreds of men at work, locomotive engines, horses, iron wagons, cranes and winches, all in motion.

By then the work had reached the stage where the granite circular heads of the breakwaters and the new coaling and landing wharves were in a state of near completion.

The work was not without its dangers. A south easterly gale on the night of 8 October 1854 caused some sixty feet of temporary staging to be carried away by the sea. Gales damaged the timber supports of the breakwater in November 1859, and in January 1860 a trainload of stone fell into the sea from a temporary bridge over the southern entrance. By the time the work was completed in 1872, twenty two men had died as the result of accidents and five had been drowned. Yet even as the works progressed as many as a hundred vessels at a time sought refuge behind them in winter storms.

By the end of 1862 there was already a wall of stone nearly a mile and a half long, nearly a hundred feet high above the sea bed and three hundred feet thick at its base. Six million tons of stone had been used. The gap in the wall was wide enough to allow two line of battle ships to pass through side by side. It also enabled sailing vessels to pass out into smooth waters in a northerly wind and proceed down channel without having to beat up the whole length of the breakwater. On the eastern end of the breakwater, overlooking the gap, was a small circular granite fort mounting eight guns that commanded the entrance. The superstructure of the great northern breakwater fort at the outer extremity had not been started, though the wooden scaffolding was in position to carry the trains loaded with stones. The tramway had to carry heavy loads and also to resist the heavy seas that broke across it. The trains brought sixty to eighty tons of stone to a steam traveller that swung two or three wagons in a wide circle to the point on the structure where the stone was to be deposited. When completed the fort would mount heavy and light batteries and have its own small dock.

The defences of the harbour of refuge included batteries at the Verne Citadel, two batteries at Dirdale Point and Blacknor Point respectively. The Nothe Fort, at the entrance to Weymouth harbour was, by 1869, a casemated granite fortress, designed for ten heavy guns protected by iron shields, together with two light guns sited to overlook the Weymouth entrance. The eastern side of Verne Hill had six batteries with 27 guns sited at heights above sea level varying from 150 feet to 234 feet. The flank guns of these batteries were mounted to use the Moncrieff system, whereby a gun could be hoisted above the parapet for firing, when the recoil would cause it to run back into the gunpit. It could then be loaded in safety by the gun detachment.

The last stone of the breakwater was deposited on Saturday 3 March 1871 and in the following month a fleet steamed through the southern entrance for the first time. The following year the Queen declared her intention of giving a knighthood to John Coode for his

The Moncrieff gun carriage was used with some Portland guns. After firing, the gun swung back below the parapet. The gun could then be reloaded in the comparative shelter of the gun pit.

SULTAN. HERCULES. MINOTAUR. HECTOR. PENELOPE. AGINCOURT
VANGUARD. RESISTANCE. NORTHUMBERLAND. AUDACIOUS. BLACK-PRINCE.
VALIANT. BELLEROPHON. FAVOURITE.

THE GRAND REVIEW OF THE **COMBINED CHANNEL & RESERVE SQUADRONS**
BEFORE H.R.H. THE PRINCE OF WALES *ON THE OCCASION OF HIS LAYING THE LAST STONE ON THE COMPLETION*
OF THE PORTLAND BREAKWATER. AUG. 10. 1872.

twenty five years service. The breakwater was officially opened by the Prince of Wales on 18 August 1872. A stone carried the inscription:-

> From this spot, on 25 July 1849, His Royal Highness Prince Albert, consort of Queen Victoria, sank the first stone of this breakwater. Upon the same spot, Albert Edward, Prince of Wales, on 18 August 1872 laid this last stone and declared the works complete. These are imperial works and worthy kings.

As a harbour of refuge, Portland soon demonstrated its value. Merchant vessels and men of war sheltered and assembled within the protection of the breakwater. At first it seemed that there was no intention of providing a naval base. The Royal Commission on Defences in the United Kingdom reported in 1860:-

> There are no naval establishments at Portland and we are informed that there is at present no intention of constructing any.

It went on to say that:-

> if it ever be decided to provide storehouses and other appliances for refitting and provisioning a fleet at this station, it will be impossible, by any works of fortification, to protect the harbour from bombardment, owing to the salient position of Portland.

Nevertheless the protection now offered did allow ships to remain there on a more permanent basis. In 1862 a training ship, the *Britannia*, arrived, but within a few months adverse reports appeared in *The Times* and the *United Services Gazette*, claiming that Portland was unsuitable for the training of cadets, some of whom had suffered 'considerable seasickness' since the ship had been there. Despite denials of these charges in the House of Commons, it was decided to transfer the ship to Dartmouth, where the name *Britannia* remains to this day as the Royal Naval College. The ship sailed from Portland on 29 September 1863.

The training ship BOSCAWEN at her moorings in Portland harbour. Beyond her lies the old broadside ironclad MINOTAUR, relegated to training duties as BOSCAWEN II. They served at Portland until 1905.

HMS Boscawen

In October 1866 another training ship, the three decker *Boscawen*, arrived in Portland Roads, towed from Spithead by the wooden paddle frigate *Gladiator*. The local press announced that there would be vacancies aboard for twenty lads:

> who must be over 14½, and not above 16 years: 4′8″ tall if 14½ or 15 with not less than 27″ chest: to be able to read and write fairly, strong, healthy, well grown, active and intelligent, free from all physical malformation, must be able to pass a strict medical examination by the surgeon of the ship; must never have had fits.

Written consent was required from parents, together with a birth certificate, and the boys had to go for examination at their own expense.

Under Commander H Fairfax, the boy cadets engaged in making and mending clothes, scrubbing and washing clothes, cleaning decks, furling sails, scrubbing hammocks, sail drill and rifle drill. Boys were sent on shore, but they could on occasion be forced to remain on board on account of threatening weather, or if the boys had an infectious disease like measles.

Just as had happened with HMS *Britannia*, criticism mounted over keeping HMS *Boscawen* at Portland. There was a threat to send her to Southampton, but a petition supported by Captain Manning, Her Majesty's Lieutenant of the Isle of Portland, and John Tizard, Mayor of Weymouth, was successful, and the training ship was present at the opening of the breakwater in 1872, the ship's company and cadets crowding the yards and rigging. Five brigs, also used for cadet training, attended the ceremony. So the *Boscawen* remained at Portland and became part of the growing naval use of the harbour of refuge.

The first *Boscawen*, built as a third rate of 70 guns, had served in the Baltic Fleet in 1854. She left her role as training ship at Portland, was renamed *Wellesley*, and replaced by the first rate *Trafalgar* in 1873. HMS *Trafalgar*, built in 1841, had served in the Black Sea, the Mediterranean and the English Channel before being converted into a boys' training ship at Portsmouth in 1869. On coming to Portland she was renamed *Boscawen* as the boys' training ship at the base.

Boys of HMS BOSCAWEN scrubbing boats.

In 1882 a boys' training establishment was set up on the eastern slopes of Portland as an instructional depot for the three decker. Ten years later it was commissioned as a separate command which took the name *Boscawen* and became a gunnery training establishment for men and boys from warships in the harbour. This arrangement continued until April 1907, when the *Boscawen* was relieved by the cruiser *Sapphire* under the command of Captain Walter Cowan. Between 1893 and 1905, two old battleships, *Minotaur* and *Agincourt* were based at Portland as part of HMS *Boscawen*. They were known as *Boscawen II* and *Boscawen III* respectively. When the ceremony of the laying of the last stone of the breakwater took place in 1872, these two ships had been present as first class units of the Channel Fleet.

Cadets from the various naval training establishments continued to receive sail training, even at the turn of the century. By this time the fleet was steam driven. But still the brigs, including *Seaflower* and *Martin* came to Portland. Admiral of the Fleet, Lord Cunningham, among others, has recorded his early sea experiences as a young midshipman aboard these ships. Discipline was strict, even harsh. But a proposal to abolish the caning of boy seamen in 1906 drew from the Dorset County Chronicle a firm condemnation of such a retrograde step:

Lads come from all over the country with ideas of equality in their heads, and old hands would wonder how they are to be punished for their numerous breaches of discipline.

Early Experiments and Sea Trials

The shelter and facilities of the harbour enabled the Royal Navy to carry out some experimental work at Portland. The Channel Fleet had already become a frequent visitor when, in July 1872, experiments were carried out to discover the effects of gunfire on a warship's turret. For this purpose the ironclad ram *Hotspur* was to fire a 600lb shot from her 25 ton gun at the new single turret monitor

The training brig SEAFLOWER gave many naval cadets their first taste of life at sea.

Glatton. Firing was to be carried out at a range of 200 yards. The *Glatton* was moored about one mile from Portland inside the breakwater and 200 feet from the harbour wall. She was moored with bow anchors and stern cable, her head pointing across Weymouth Bay towards Osmington Mills. The *Hotspur* was directly opposite and 200 yards distant. Lords of the Admiralty were present and the shrouds of the training ship *Boscawen* were 'black with boys and men'. *Hotspur's* first shot missed, but the second and third shots struck *Glatton's* turret. The mechanism of the turret was not damaged. This was proved by the firing of four sighting shots. It was subsequently reported that a goat, fowl and other animals placed inside the turret 'did not appear in the least concerned at their positions'.

One of the first seagoing 'mastless' turret ships, HMS *Thunderer*, completed in May 1877, was at Portland for trials from July to November. Her steam pinnace was used for experimental work, including the firing of torpedoes. She also carried out turning trials off the breakwater to obtain the angle of heel. Commanded by Captain J C Wilson, the *Thunderer's* Executive Officer was Commander Lord Charles Beresford, already a Member of Parliament and destined to become Commander in Chief, Channel Fleet. While a serving officer aboard the *Thunderer*, he spoke in the House of Commons on 19 March, saying, even before the ship's completion:

> We may manufacture guns and build very powerful ships, but the nation with the best torpedoes will win the next war.

The *Thunderer's* log indicates the activities at Portland during the Autumn of 1877. HMS *Resistance* was observed passing up the Channel. The flagship of the Channel Fleet *Minotaur* entered the Roads as well as the *Black Prince*, flagship of the second in command, the *Defence* of the Channel Fleet, the *Warrior*, guardship of the Portland coastguard district, the wooden gun vessel *Griffon*, the training brig *Seaflower* and a Norwegian frigate. The *Defence* with the Trinity yacht *Galatea* towed the wreck of the two decker *Forest* into Portland late in September, following the *Forest's* disastrous collision with the iron sailing ship *Avalanche* about two weeks earlier.

The Torpedo

The invention of the torpedo had a considerable impact upon Portland. Although the new weapon immediately exposed the inadequate protection provided by the original breakwater, it was in due time manufactured and tested within the newly extended enclosed harbour and the waters of Weymouth Bay.

In 1867, work by Captain Luppis of the Austrian Navy and a British engineer, Robert Whitehead, had led to the production in Italy of the first self propelled torpedo. In January of that year the Foreign Office received a letter from one Charles Thomas Hill in Fiume. It referred to a weapon with the capacity:

> to completely destroy any vessel of war passing or at anchor by its contact when so directed, and launched from the shore, or from vessels afloat. The machine is self propelled with necessary force and has speed under the water's surface at some six feet depth, less or more so as to be perfectly invisible to the enemy advancing; and when on its contact with the object it explodes and destruction is complete all round.

The weapon was further developed and produced at the Whitehead factory at Fiume. In 1869 Robert Whitehead brought two of the torpedoes to England where they were given trials at Sheerness. The success of one of these torpedoes in sinking its target led the Admiralty to adopt the Whitehead torpedo for the Royal Navy. A committee under Vice-Admiral Sir Alexander Milne KCB reported:

> that ships fitted to fire the Whitehead torpedo would greatly add to the power of the fleet: that torpedo tubes fitted beneath the surface to coast batteries would materially assist in the defence of narrow passages especially where, as in the case of most of our rivers, the amount of navigation would be a serious obstacle to the use of fixed

floating torpedoes, and that there would be value in torpedoes fitted for boat service.

The Admiralty was only prepared to buy these torpedoes if they were built in Britain. As a result a factory was built at Wyke Regis between Portland and Weymouth and opened in 1891. It was managed by Captain E.P.Gallwey, an associate of Robert Whitehead, who continued to develop the weapon. The new factory bordered on Portland harbour and a long pier was built projecting into the harbour for testing torpedoes completed at the factory.

pedoes, of 14 inch and 18 inch diameter were much improved in 1910 when a heater was perfected which doubled the speed and increased the range of the torpedo by heating the compressed air within it. There were hazards in having a test range within a working harbour and there were several occasions when ships, particularly merchantmen that had come in for coaling, were narrowly missed or even struck by practice torpedoes. These weapons were fortunately without their warheads. The practice of sounding a whistle and hoisting a red flag gave warning to all in the

Whitehead's Torpedo Factory. The long Torpedo Pier and the seaplane have probably been added to give the picture more dramatic appeal.

Before the end of the century naval warfare had been revolutionised and the power of the torpedo demonstrated. A Turkish vessel was sunk by the Russians in Bakum harbour in 1878; during the Chilean revolution the rebel battleship *Blanco Encalada* was sunk at anchor by two Chinese gunboats; in 1895 the Japanese destroyed four Chinese warships at We-Hai-Wei; and in 1905 the torpedoes of Japanese warships finally annihilated the Russian fleet after the Battle of Tsushima.

At Weymouth the only customer of the new factory was the British Admiralty, but production was steadily established and skilled labour came to the area. Then in 1905 and again in 1909 orders were placed by the United States of America. These early tor-

harbour that a practice shoot was about to take place, but even so the warnings sometimes went unnoticed or unheeded.

Numbers of Whitehead torpedoes were lost when launched from the forward firing tubes of battleships and cruisers. Practice was therefore discontinued in 1896 in all vessels other than torpedo boats and destroyers. Efficiency was to be maintained by "going through the motions of firing". The Fiume model of the torpedo was withdrawn the next year from service because of its erratic behaviour and some 1300 torpedoes were destroyed.

Ill fortune befell the Whitehead family and the company. Robert Whitehead himself retired because of ill health in the late nineties and died in 1905. His son John died in 1902, his close associate Count George Hoyos died in 1904, and finally, Captain Gallwey, manager of the Weymouth factory, died in 1906. The Admiralty, aware that this succession of events put the company's future in jeopardy, approached the two great armament engineering firms Vickers Ltd and Sir W G Armstrong, Whitworth & Co Ltd, who agreed to buy control of the Whitehead company between them. English law required that a new company be established and this was formed in January 1907 as Whitehead Torpedo Works (Weymouth) Ltd. It produced torpedoes for the Royal Navy for the next fourteen years before going into voluntary liquidation in 1921 as a result of the slump in demand for the weapon after the end of the First World War. But two years later the factory reopened. By this time there was a 21 inch torpedo. Modernisation of the plant followed in 1934 with a capacity to produce at least 250 torpedoes a year. There were contracts from Brazil, China, Greece, Holland, Poland and Turkey as well as the Royal Navy. In 1939 the factory produced 492 torpedoes.

The Royal Navy established a Torpedo Depot in the dockyard in 1901, but this was transferred across the harbour to Bincleaves during the First World War. Workshops were built there with a short torpedo range operating within the harbour. The Admiralty Long Torpedo Range and a Whitehead Torpedo Range shared a structure pointing from Bincleaves Groyne out into Weymouth Bay.

2

ENCLOSING THE HARBOUR

Hardly had the southern breakwater and its granite fort been completed than the invention of the torpedo and development of long range guns left the harbour exposed to attack. In particular, fast small torpedo carrying surface vessels could launch their weapons against exposed battleships and armoured cruisers at anchor in the harbour. A report on United Kingdom Harbours by Sir John Rennie in 1854 had stated:

The importance of Portland, not only as a station and port of refuge for ships of war, but for the immense numbers of mercantile vessels which pass and re-pass on their route to and from the Atlantic to London and other ports, and its proximity to France being only 60 miles distant, make it extremely desirable that such further artificial protection should be given to it to make it perfectly secure against gales from the East which is the only quarter to which it is exposed.

The Admiralty was particularly concerned when the French established a number of torpedo stations along the coast from Brest to Dunkirk with the intention of harrassing Channel shipping in the event of war. Torpedo boats would very likely sail at night and make anchorages along the English side of the Channel untenable. The British response was to include simulated torpedo attacks in the fleet manoeuvres of 1890. A flotilla of torpedo boats was based at Alderney for the exercise and two squadrons of ironclads and their supporting ships were ordered to defend Channel trade. The torpedo boats, led by Commander J Barry and Lieutenant F C D Sturdee, entered fully into the offensive spirit of the torpedo boat flotillas and attacked Admiral Sir George Tryon's fleet while it was still anchored in Plymouth Sound. In order to escape them, the Admiral was forced to take his ships to the Scilly Isles, thus leaving the English Channel he was supposed to defend at the mercy of the marauding torpedo boats.

The disposition of the French torpedo boats along the northern coast of France and the experience of the 1890 manoeuvres, convinced the Admiralty that something must be done

Battleships of the MAJESTIC class, with attendant cruisers, protected by the southern arm of the Portland breakwater. Part of the Channel Fleet, the ships are painted black with white upperworks and buff funnels. The line of dolphins in the distance mark the temporary protection of the ships against torpedo attack until the harbour is fully enclosed. Photograph c. 1898.

The battleship NEPTUNE lies close to the partially completed Loading Jetty and the Camber Jetty. Between the jetties the slipway that was adapted in 1917 to take seaplanes can be seen.

to protect warships at their anchorages. Already the Russian War Scare of 1885 had demonstrated how vulnerable a British Fleet might be to torpedo attack. In that year a Particular Service Squadron was formed and assembled at Portland ready to undertake the duties of a Baltic Expeditionary Force. The motley collection of ships consisted of twelve ironclad battleships, four of them with turrets and the other eight firing broadside, five assorted cruisers, a torpedo boat carrier, a sloop, six gunboats and the strange looking torpedo ram *Polyphemus*. There was great anxiety over the protection of these ships from Russian—and possibly French—torpedo boats. Fortunately war was averted by diplomacy. The assembled ships therefore exercised together, paying particular attention to their various needs in defence against torpedo attacks. In September, Captain J A Fisher, later to become First Sea Lord, and at this time in command of the ironclad *Minotaur,* was engaged in exercises with torpedo boats at Weymouth.

It was after the war scare of 1885 and the manoeuvres of 1890 that the First Naval Lord argued for the construction of defences at Portland and Dover. He also called for the development of a torpedo boat catcher, or, as

it came to be called, a torpedo boat destroyer.

At Portland the necessary work began with the construction of additional breakwaters to enclose the harbour. This took some years to complete and in the meantime a line of dolphins made of iron and wood with nets between them was placed in position as a temporary defence. Though bad weather delayed construction, the two new breakwaters had been brought to low water mark by April 1899, five months ahead of schedule. As before, stone was quarried, weighed and sent down the inclined railway. Work was carried out by contract labour and the contractors, Messrs W Hill & Co negotiated with the Admiralty that a bonus of £1250 would be paid for every month saved on the four and a quarter years allowed for the completion of the work, though it was also agreed that the total bonus should not exceed £7500. The contractor's diary recorded that six horses and 700 men were employed daily in unloading and depositing rubble stone, repairing tools, plant and roadways, levelling beds and forming parapets. On a good day 1500 tons of stone were deposited. At night a small gang about 27 men was employed on the works.

The growth of the steam driven fleet and its demand for coal led to a coaling station being

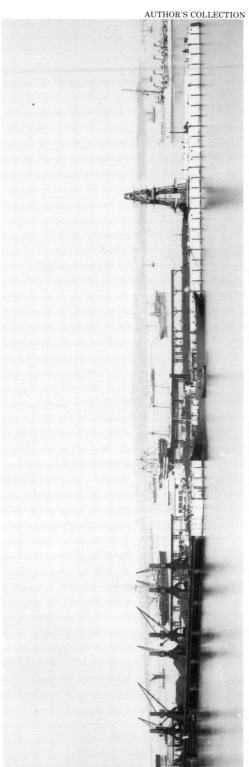

The coaling jetty was extended in 1906. The training ship BOSCAWEN is visible beyond the jetty. The light cruiser on the right is probably HMS ATTENTIVE while the vessel behind the cranes may be IMPERIEUSE which became a destroyer depot ship in 1905 and was based at Portland under the name SAPPHIRE II. She reverted to her original name in 1909.

This photograph, taken in March 1906, shows the extended Coaling Jetty.

The Torpedo Boat Destroyer pens taken from the coaling jetty looking south west towards Chesil Beach. (March 1906).

Looking to the North East. (March 1906).

completed at Portland in 1895. As early as 1868, in response to a question in the House of Commons, the Secretary of the Admiralty reported that "Welsh coal fields could be brought into communication with the inner breakwater at Portland". This could be achieved with the co-operation of the Great Western and South Western Railways. Portland therefore virtually became the headquarters of the Channel Fleet. High quality Welsh coal was brought to the coaling depot; in November 1899 an order was placed for 150,000 tons of steam coal at 19 shillings a ton—"the highest price paid by the Admiralty".

By 1906 the new breakwaters had been completed and the harbour of refuge became a busy naval anchorage. The occupation of a large part of the anchorage by the Royal Navy meant that its use by merchant ships was restricted, though they continued to take on coal from the hulks moored in the harbour. The naval coaling pier had just come into operation with its two coal tips and six hydraulic cranes. Oil tanks were being constructed to refuel the new oil burning warships. The first two oil tanks, built on The Common in 1901 were followed by others at The Mere until there were twenty six in all. Wooden pens were completed for the torpedo boats and destroyers. A hospital, new canteen, recreation grounds and three official residences all combined to establish Portland as a permanent base for His Majesty's ships. In 1909, the seaward side of the outer breakwater was raised 11 feet by cutting away the inner position and placing the stone on top of the outer position.

Employees at the dockyard started work at 0700, and since no trains ran to Portland earlier than 0800, those men living at Weymouth or even as far away as Chickerell or Upwey had to walk to work in all weathers for wages of nineteen shillings a week.

Harbour Defences

Further consideration now had to be given to the defence of the harbour against enemy attack. A conference between the Admiralty and the War Office in November 1903 reported to the Cabinet on the strategic conditions governing the coast defences of the United Kingdom as affected by naval considerations. It was thought that naval attack against fortified ports was improbable. On the other hand the ports in southern England were within easy reach of enemy naval squadrons and raids were always a possibility.

It seemed that a torpedo attack at night was most likely, particularly in the early stages of a war. For that reason, arrangements must be made to provide 'electric lighting' at the five naval ports of Medway, Dover, Portsmouth, Portland and Plymouth. Larger vessels, it was thought, would be unlikely to attack defended ports at night and therefore medium and heavy artillery would most likely be required by daylight, whereas the quick-firing guns and machine guns would probably be employed in thick weather or after dark. The Committee of Imperial Defence set up a Home Ports Defence Committee in 1909 to advise on the co-operation of the Navy and the Army for the defence of home ports as well as regulating the traffic there.

The Committee on Armaments of Home Ports reported on Portland in 1905. It believed that the two 9.2 inch guns of the East Weares battery and the two 9.2 inch guns at Upton were sufficient to repel an attack by cruisers from the east or south. A cruiser might, however, lie to the west of Chesil Bank and shell Portland harbour by direct fire from a position exposed only to the fire of the six 9 inch guns of the Verne battery and the two 12.5 inch muzzle loading guns of the Verne citadel. The committee recommended that two 9.2 inch guns should be mounted on the site of the Blacknor battery instead of the existing 6 inch and that the older guns of the Verne Citadel and Verne Quarry should be removed. It seemed most likely that, like Dover, Portland would be especially exposed to the attack of 'blockers' and 'boom smashers'. Strong defences were therefore required to protect the entrances to the har-

Despite some local objections, the foundations are prepared for the oil fuel tanks at The Mere, Portland.

. . . Inside the tanks . . .

Torpedo boats at their trots with the Whitehead torpedo works pier in the background.

bour. Boom defences as well as guns must be installed.

The Committee recommended the following guns as necessary for the defence of the harbour:

Breakwater Fort:

   i.   the four 12.5 inch muzzle loading guns were useless.

   ii.   two 6 inch breech loading guns would be placed on top of the breakwater fort, in place of the existing four 12 pdr quick firing guns as anti-torpedo boat defence.

   iii.   two 6 inch breech loading guns in embrasures would be sited to fire with a north easterly arc.

East Weares:

      three 6 inch breech loading guns would reinforce the two 9.2 inch guns, all of which would be manned at night.

Nothe Fort:

   i.   three 6 inch breech loading guns were needed, two of which were already in position, but the third should be added.

   ii.   the two 6 pdr guns were useless.

Lighting was regarded as important, with concentrated searchlights on the Breakwater Fort and the Nothe, two searchlights to act as fighting lights for the East Weares battery, and the light already at Bincleaves should be brought forward onto the breakwater to illuminate the northern entrance.

Procedures had already been established for the operation of an examination service. There would be two examination vessels, *Spey* and *Spanker*, under the command of Commander Louis F C Jackson RN. Additional ships listed for the examination service outside Portland harbour were the Cosens paddle steamers *Queen* and *Albert Victor*, and the privately owned Portland tugs *Verne* and *Hector*. Their purpose was to prevent the entry of hostile ships into the waters leading to the ports of Portland and Weymouth "whether by force, treachery or strategem". The 'examination line' was set from the Breakwater Fort, North 18 degrees west to the opposite shore. Admiral A K Wilson, Commander in Chief, Channel Fleet, expressed the view that there was a risk of entrances to Portland being blocked by the enemy sinking ships in them. No merchant ships, therefore, except those attending the Fleet should be allowed to pass in wartime inside a line drawn from Portland Bill to the Shambles and from the Shambles to the Whitenose Fort. With the existing line, Wilson thought that a ship might almost get to the entrance before being stopped.

By the outbreak of war in 1914, an enclosed and defended harbour had largely been achieved.

3

THE FLEET AT PORTLAND 1900—1914

A view looking across the Bincleaves Torpedo Pier. A fleet of battleships and cruisers fill the harbour.

From the turn of the century, the upper-works of great warships towered above the grey stone walls of the breakwaters. On the battleships and cruisers the masts carrying the new wireless aerials stood tall and thin against the sky, and the coal burning ships with two, three or four funnels belched smoke as they raised steam after the filthy task of coaling ship in which the whole ship's company joined. The oil burning ships, newer and cleaner, took their places in the teeming anchorage. In company with the battle fleets came the light scouting cruisers and the fussy, protective destroyers. Week by week the visits of ships were reported in the local newspapers, and day by day the training programmes were prepared. By 1904 the Admiralty had decided to concentrate its most powerful ships in home waters by the establishment of a Home Fleet as well as a Channel Fleet. The Channel Fleet was initially made up of twelve battleships, four of which had been withdrawn from the Mediterranean. The next year five more battleships were brought from the China Station. Meanwhile a newly created Atlantic Fleet with eight of the latest battleships had Gibraltar as the permanent base from which it could reinforce the Mediterranean and the Channel Fleets. Squadrons of armoured cruisers were attached to each fleet.

An Admiralty memorandum of 1906 declared that Germany was the only potential enemy and it was decided to reorganise the fleets once more. A more powerful Home Fleet was established by withdrawing ships from the Mediterranean, Gibraltar and from other fleets based in British home waters. This very powerful force was based at Portland with two supplementary bases at the Nore and Berehaven. It was attended by its destroyer flotillas. In the year 1906 it was reported that some 180 warships and 85 torpedo boat destroyers used the harbour facilities. The ships exercised drills in coaling, painting and cleaning ship, anti-torpedo evolutions, use of sea boat's crew, darkening ship, collison stations and gunnery.

It was to meet the needs of the ships' companies of the battle fleet and its supporting ships that more facilities were developed not only in Portland but also in Weymouth. Sailors came ashore in their hundreds from the ships, brought into Weymouth in tenders and sometimes by paddle steamers. Many public houses opened in the town, and to deal with the consequences of over indulgence, premises were taken in the town for use as a picket house at a rent of one shilling a year. The Admiralty promised to keep the premises clean and in good order. With the King and Prince of Wales as patrons, a Sailors' Home was officially opened by Lord Tweedmouth, the First Lord, in February 1907. Naval officers present included Captain Cradock of HMS *Swiftsure*, Captain C E Anson of the cruiser *Argyll*, Captain Sir Robert Arbuthnot of the *Hampshire* and Captain Walter Cowan of the *Sapphire*.

Gunnery practice was a regular feature of the ships' programmes. In 1906 the obsolete cruiser *Landrail* was a target for the battleships *Exmouth, Albermarle, Triumph* and *Prince George. Landrail* had been filled with cork, empty barrels and ashes, and was moored in West Bay. Firing began at 7000 yards and the ships steamed at 16 knots until the range was reduced to 3000 yards. After the exercise the *Landrail* sank while under tow.

The period from 1900 until the outbreak of war in 1914 was one of growing reaction against the apathy towards gunnery practice borne of over confidence and a long period of peace. Captain, later Rear Admiral, Percy Scott was one who constantly advocated training to improve accuracy, range and rate of fire. He was aboard the battleship *Exmouth* in 1906, and as Rear Admiral commanding the Second Cruiser Squadron in the *Good Hope* was serving with the Channel Fleet a year later. Here he was the centre of

controversy arising out of the growing bitterness and rivalry between Admiral Sir John Fisher, the First Sea Lord, and Admiral Lord Charles Beresford, Commander in Chief of the Channel Fleet. While exercising at Portland, Scott received a signal from Beresford that his squadron was to return to harbour and paint ship for a review by the Kaiser. Scott was not at all pleased at the interruption to gunnery practice. In response to a signal from the *Roxburgh*, a cruiser in his squadron, he signalled:

> As paintwork appears to be more important than gunnery you are to return to harbour and make yourselves look pretty.

The Commander in Chief came to hear of this signal, summoned Scott to his flagship and gave him a thorough dressing down in the presence of other flag officers. He then sent a general signal to the fleet outlining the circumstances and ordering Scott to remove the offending signal from the log both of the *Good Hope* and *Roxburgh*. Beresford reported the matter to the Admiralty who, though expressing 'grave disapprobation', did no more to support the Admiral. Since Fisher as First Sea Lord had appointed Scott, Beresford believed that he was involved in the entire episode. Hostility between Fisher and Beresford and their respective supporters became more open and affected the efficiency of the Navy. Officers tended to support one camp or the other and the rivalry distracted them from more important matters. Scott is reported as saying of Beresford, who was a Member of Parliament as well as a serving officer:

> In the navy we knew he was not a sailor but thought he was a politician; in the House of Commons, I have been told, they knew he was not a politician but thought he was a sailor.

Gunnery practice had its critics ashore in Dorset. The Reverend W Bond of the village of Tyneham complained to the Admiralty of the shaking of homes caused by heavy firing from the battleship *Triumph* in August 1906. The vibrations were caused when the ship was out in Weymouth Bay and the village

Admiral Lord Charles Beresford, C-in-C Channel Fleet, aboard his flagship at Portland.

The battleship TRIUMPH lies at anchor with a snow covered Portland behind her. Her gunfire was later to disturb the peace of Dorset villages!

was not sheltered by the promontory at Ringstead. The Admiralty, unimpressed, replied to the complaint, concluding:

> . . . the interests of Public Service cannot be subordinated to considerations affecting individual cases.

Lord Charles Beresford's period as Commander in Chief of the Channel Fleet was not without innovation. He was concerned over the best method of sweeping mines when the fleet left harbour. On a visit to Grimsby he saw hundreds of trawlers in the harbour and, after inspecting some of the vessels and talking to their skippers he suggested a trial of two trawlers as auxiliary minesweepers. Commander E L Booty of the battleship *King Edward VII* selected two vessels, *Andes* and *Algome*. They reached Portland on 5 February 1908 and spent the next eight days sweeping up dummy mines. The success of the experiment and the knowledge gained prepared the way for trawlers and drifters to serve in large numbers as auxiliary minesweepers in the two world wars.

Apart from fleet manoeuvres at sea, there were also occasional exercises in the landing of sailors and marines on 'enemy' shores and in attacking fortifications. One such exercise

took place on 8 December 1908 with an assault on the Verne Fort. The battleship *Bulwark* and the cruiser *Drake* provided the defending force under Captain R F Scott of the *Bulwark*. For the attacking forces, Admiral Lord Charles Beresford was Commander in Chief, Naval Forces; Rear Admiral James Startin was in charge of the Field Guns; Vice Admiral Sir Berkeley Milne commanded the Infantry Brigades. The first Brigade was under Captain J M de Robeck, the Second under Captain the Hon. H H Hood, the Third under Captain A C Leverson and the Fourth under Major A M Hire of the Royal Marines.

Captain Scott, as an explorer, later led the ill-fated expedition to the South Pole. Berkeley Milne, de Robeck and Leverson all achieved high office, de Robeck being much involved with the naval side of the Dardanelles campaign in 1915. Hood was killed aboard his flagship *Invincible*, leading his battle cruiser squadron into action at the Battle of Jutland in 1916.

The guns were landed and hauled to the heights, the naval brigades moved forward under cover, one marine brigade sounding the charge and dashing forward to capture a

27

howitzer battery. Before the exercise began it was arranged that the attack should be repulsed so that the attacking brigades could practise an orderly withdrawal. During the retirement down the steep hillsides, the Commander in Chief noticed that many men had their ammunition pouches open, and cartridges were being lost, which would have been most serious in real warfare. The exercise ended with four brigades and field gun batteries marching past Lord Charles Beresford at Castletown, while two brigades marched past Vice-Admiral Sir Berkeley Milne at the bottom of the inclined railway. The mock assault over, the men returned to their ships.

number of naval personnel stood at 68. The cemetery, on the hill overlooking the harbour, was transferred to the Admiralty in 1907 and was extended in 1914 "for the interment of persons of His Majesty's service, whether naval, military or civil, and the members of their families who shall die in or near Portland."

While injuries and some deaths occurred among the naval personnel, there were a number of accidents, some minor but others serious, that caused damage to HM ships and sometimes brought down the wrath of Their Lordships upon the officer responsible. The Portsmouth Command Accident Book listed such occurrences. Damage was caused to a

A full house in the destroyer pens. It is easy to see how accidents occurred.

The intense and continuous activity of the Royal Navy at Portland, and the ever present risks and dangers inherent when men are engaged in the maintenance of a complicated war machine like a warship, meant that there were accidents and casualties, some of them resulting in death.

A military cemetery had been established at Portland in 1876 and there had been a number of fatalities while the Verne was a military fortification. But by 1907 the number of army burials had declined while the number of naval burials had increased. Between 1898 and 1907 there were 28 army burials and 87 naval, while between 1907 and 1912 there were only 6 army burials but the

number of torpedo boat destroyers in coming alongside the destroyer pens when propellers struck the wooden piles or a hidden obstruction. Plating could also be damaged going alongside another ship or a jetty. There were occasions when anchor cables parted and anchors were lost, and there were collisions and groundings. No ship was lost, and considering the number of warship movements, the accident toll was commendably light.

While the battleship HMS *Dreadnought*, flagship of Admiral Sir William May, Commander in Chief Home Fleet, was in Portland Roads, she was the scene of a famous hoax. On 7 February 1910, three young men and a young lady, dressed as the Emperor and

Princes of Abyssinia, were officially welcomed aboard the ship. They were accompanied by a so-called Foreign Office official and a German interpreter to the princes. The 'Abyssinians' were dressed with silk sashes as turbans, rich robes and jewels, and tapered oriental boots. Arriving by train they were given 'red carpet' treatment and subsequently spent an hour on a state visit to the

Fleets assembled in Portland harbour and in Weymouth Bay for review. Sometimes the Home and Atlantic fleets combined, as in May 1912, for a royal review by King George V. The King was due to arrive on 7 May but ships assembled several days before that. When the battleship *Collingwood* arrived on the morning of 2 May two divisions of battleships and two cruiser squadrons were already

The fleet at anchor off Weymouth (1912) awaiting the Royal review.

flagship. Though the cousin of one of the young men was an officer aboard the *Dreadnought*, they were not recognised. As students from Cambridge, they had already perpetrated at least one other hoax. The young lady, Virginia Stephen, later became the novelist Virginia Woolf.

A Short S 27 hydroplane takes off from the battleship HIBERNIA with Portland visible in the distance. Flights were made from the ship in May 1912 by Commander Samson and Lieutenant Gregory.

at anchor. The battleship *Hibernia*, arriving before noon, carried aeroplanes aboard, mounted on a platform over the forward turret that extended the length of the forecastle. The first machine, piloted by Commander Samson, flew from the ship to land on the east side of Weymouth. The next day he flew round the fleet and landed close to the battleship *Neptune*. The aircraft was fitted with floats to enable it to land on the water.

The day before the King was due, ships already at Portland put to sea and were joined by the Atlantic Fleet. The combined fleets formed up and anchored in review order before dressing overall and firing a royal salute of twenty-one guns to commemorate the accession of King George V to the throne.

It was then that the weather intervened. The Royal Yacht was forced to remain fog bound at Yarmouth, so the King did not arrive as expected. However, Winston Churchill, the First Lord of the Admiralty, with the First Sea Lord in the Admiralty yacht *Enchantress* inspected the fleet. Churchill then took a short trip in the submarine D4. Though the Royal Yacht arrived on 8 May, the fog caused the day's programme to be cancelled. But on Thursday 9

The Destroyer depot ship IMPERIEUSE at Portland between 1905 and 1909. Built as an armoured cruiser in 1883, she originally had a peacetime sailing rig for economical cruising. Her early years were spent on the China Station and in the Pacific.

May the weather cleared enough to enable twelve battleships of the 1st and 2nd Battle Squadrons to put to sea for firing practice. The King was aboard the Battleship *Neptune*, while Churchill, Asquith and Balfour were in another battleship, the *Orion*. Soon after the *Neptune* opened fire the fog closed in once more and the ships returned to Weymouth Bay. Later in the day the fog once more lifted enough to enable two aeroplanes to fly round the fleet. More successful firing took place the next day though only at short range. During this shoot, a world record was claimed when the *Orion* with her ten 13.5 inch guns made 21 hits out of 28 rounds at a range of 6000 yards.

The King left Weymouth on the morning of 11 May after which the 1st and 2nd Battle Squadrons entered Portland Harbour and moored.

Portland was frequently visited by warships of foreign powers. The new Japanese battleship *Fuji*, built in Britain at the Thames Iron works, visited Portland in 1897. While at anchor in the harbour a quick-firing gun aboard the battleship *Prince George* discharged a live round between the funnels of the Japanese ship causing 'considerable confusion'. A Russian squadron called for coaling in 1902 and in 1913 ships of their Baltic Fleet entered the harbour, being saluted by the battleship *Dreadnought*. The powerful Russian squadron included the battleships *Cesarevic, Slava, Andrej Pervozvannyj, Imperator Pavel I*, the cruisers *Rurik, Admiral Makarov, Bajan, Pallada* and *Gromoboj*, the transport *Riga* and four destroyers.

Ships of the United States Navy were in the English Channel in 1910. The British battleship *Britannia* passed an American squadron south west of the Shambles that included the battleships USS *Connecticut* (flagship), *Delaware, Wisconsin* and *Michigan*, while in December the First Division of the United States Fleet, led by the flagship *Louisiana*, sailed from Cherbourg to visit Portland. A French squadron of eighteen ships visited the base in June 1914.

The Russian Battleship ANDREJ PERVOZVANNYJ visited Portland in 1913.

The Japanese battleship FUJI. A practice shot was accidentally fired between her funnels while she was at Portland. Such events are not unknown in modern times. . .

4

THE FIRST WORLD WAR

The early years of the twentieth century saw a change in the balance of power in Europe. The Anglo-French Entente in 1904 settled a number of colonial disputes between the two countries. It did not lead directly to any treaty before war broke out, but a greater understanding grew up between the two nations. France was already an ally of Russia, but understanding between Britain and Russia was never so close as that with France; nevertheless, spheres of influence were agreed in August 1907. These understandings were tested on two occasions over Morocco, when Germany, who had earlier declared no interest in that country, suddenly insisted upon its independence from France and Spain. Though this crisis was resolved by a conference at Algeciras in 1906, peace was threatened by the incident at Agadir in 1911 when the German gunboat *Panther* was sent to the port to protect German interests. Britain was already sensitive to the growth of German naval power and felt threatened by German naval rivalry. The appearance of a German gunboat close to the naval base at Gibraltar and important trade routes reinforced this concern.

The system of alliances and rival camps that had become established by 1914 meant that even the slightest spark might cause a chain reaction that would ignite Europe. The assassination of the Austrian Archduke Francis Ferdinand and his wife at Sarajevo on 28 June 1914 was that spark. The Austrians, believing the Serbian government to have been involved in the plot, delivered an ultimatum that Serbia could not accept. Alliances and treaties were invoked to precipitate war.

Less than two weeks after the assassination at Sarajevo, and with a growing threat of war with Germany looming over the horizon, ships of the Royal Navy began to assemble at Portland. It had been decided in the spring of 1914 that a test mobilisation would be held instead of the usual summer manoeuvres. By 10 July the warships filled the harbour under the command of Admiral Sir George Callaghan, Commander-in-Chief, Home Fleets. Reservists were invited to attend and responded with such a will that the fleet was soon in a state of mobilisation. With the object achieved, the fleet was due to disperse on 23 July, the very day that Austria delivered her ultimatum to Serbia. Orders were issued that the fleet should not disperse, and on the evening of 28 July it was ordered to proceed to its war station at Scapa Flow via the Dover Straits.

At 0700 on 29 July the ships began to leave

Ships of the fleet at Portland shortly before leaving for their war stations in August 1914. The steamer seems to be leaving harbour despite some trouble with her deck cargo!

harbour, first the light cruisers and then the battleships. The three exits from the harbour were used and the flagship *Iron Duke* was among the last to leave as the squadrons took station and headed into the open waters of the English Channel. The harbour at Portland, that had so recently teemed with ships and the coming and going of tenders and small boats, now fell quiet, and where the lights of a great fleet had blinked in the night sky, there was darkness. The fleet had gone to war. Only the battleship *Agamemnon* remained to await the arrival of the Second Fleet. Admiral Callaghan did not accompany the fleet to Scapa. Instead he was called to the Admiralty. He landed at Weymouth Pier and left by train for London. There he learned that he was to be relieved of his command and would be replaced by Admiral Sir John Jellicoe. The fleet itself sailed under the command of Vice Admiral Sir George Warrender. The ships did not turn eastwards until they were out of sight of land. As they passed up Channel they passed the French battleship *France* on an opposite course, having just landed the French President after his visit to the Czar.

At the beginning of the war Portland was classified as a "War Anchorage and Trawler Station". Home waters were divided into twenty three patrol areas of which Portland was designated Area XIII. In 1915 there were eight trawlers in the Auxiliary Patrol but by 1918 this number had risen to twenty eight in addition to yachts, drifters, motor launches and other minesweepers. A flotilla of hired paddle steamers joined the auxiliaries. Major warships used the anchorage when on passage to other theatres of war or when carrying out exercises. With these growing forces and the important operational work carried on from Portland, an officer of flag rank, Rear Admiral V H G Bernard CB was appointed in command. At the outbreak of war he had been captain of the battleship *Venerable*.

It seemed unlikely that the anchorage would be bombarded by large German surface warships, but since cross channel traffic with France was of vital importance, steps had to be taken to protect it from submarine torpedoes and mines. The role of the German submarines was difficult to predict and it was not known how effective they might be in wartime conditions. But at least the harbour at Portland must be made safe. In November 1914, the old turret battleship *Hood* was sunk across the southern entrance, once known as 'the hole in the wall'. The ship was manoeuvred into the gap, but instead of sinking in an upright position, she turned over and rested on her upperworks with the keel exposed at low water.

November 1914, the old battleship HOOD in position across the southern entrance to Portland harbour prior to being sunk as a blockship.

With bands playing, British sailors march to war along the Esplanade at Weymouth in September 1914.

The Loss of HMS Formidable

Early experience of the U-boats was ominous. On 22 September 1914 the three armoured cruisers *Hogue, Aboukir* and *Cressy* were sunk by one submarine, *U9*, 30 miles south of Ymuiden. By the end of the year the *Pathfinder, Hawke, Hermes* and *Niger* had all been successfully attacked by U-boats. Such was the anxiety caused by the threat of the submarines that mere suspicion of the presence of a U-boat in the English Channel brought the movement of cross channel shipping to a stop. But soon worse was to follow, and much nearer home.

Though the Grand Fleet had left Portland before war was declared, the 5th and 6th Battle Squadrons remained in Channel waters to protect the supply line to France. Some ships carried out firing exercises off Portland in turn while the rest of the force was based at Sheerness. On 30 December 1914, ships of the 5th Battle Squadron sailed for Portland for further firing practice. On 31 December the battleships *Lord Nelson,* flagship of Vice-Admiral Sir Lewis Bayly, Commander-in-Chief Channel Fleet, *Agamemnon, Queen, Implacable, Prince of Wales, Venerable, London* and *Formidable* were sailing in

line ahead, two cables apart, with the light cruisers *Topaze* and *Diamond* one mile astern. Having exercised all day, this was the night formation ordered by the Admiral. A signal was sent to Portland ordering fresh supplies to be kept for Saturday. The night, New Year's Eve, began clear but cloudy with ships visible at a distance up to two miles.

At the same time the German submarine *U24* was on patrol in the Channel. The boat had left Wilhelmshaven before Christmas and had had a relatively uneventful patrol, though a man had been washed overboard in heavy seas. Now, very early on New Year's Day 1915, icy cold and with signs of strengthening wind, a lookout on the conning tower reported smoke clouds on the starboard bow. The smoke was soon identified as coming from a squadron of battleships. The U-boat prepared to attack. In worsening sea conditions it would be difficult to keep submerged at periscope depth so it was decided to carry out the attack on the surface. Undetected, the U-boat approached until it seemed to be only a hundred metres from the battleships. A torpedo was fired at the last ship in the line.

The British squadron was quite unaware of

the presence of an enemy submarine until, at 0230, the *Formidable*, steaming at ten knots, was struck by a torpedo on the starboard side abreast of the forefunnel. She hauled out of line to port, took a list of twenty degrees and lost all steam pressure. No one knew at first whether the ship had been hit by a torpedo or had struck a mine. Three quarters of an hour later, a second torpedo struck the port side abaft the second funnel, bringing the ship onto an even keel but down by the bow. The attacking *U24* came so close in the second attack that she was forced to dive under the stricken battleship, and in doing so damaged both periscopes and the conning tower hatchway against the *Formidable's* keel. As soon as the *Formidable* was hit, the rest of the squadron altered course to the south east at

passing. The steamer signalled "I will follow you" but continued on her course, even though the battleship was firing rockets and red lights. As the *Topaze* closed the *Formidable* once more, Captain Loxley hailed: "There is a submarine on my port quarter. You can't do any good here, you had better clear out or you will be hit." The submarine was seen to pass 150 yards astern of the *Topaze*. The other light cruiser *Diamond* reported seeing the *Formidable* sink at 0439, bow first and listing to starboard. Her stern remained visible for a few minutes as the bow apparently rested on the sea bed. Thirty-seven survivors were picked up by the *Diamond* and 43 by the *Topaze*. Both ships then returned to Portland. So rough was the sea by that time and so strong the wind that

The battleship FORMIDABLE at anchor in Portland harbour. With the Sixth Battle Squadron she was due to arrive there on 1st January 1915, but early that morning was torpedoed and sunk by U 24.

16 knots for a few minutes and then turned north east at 14 knots to get well clear of danger. The night became very dark and the wind strengthened until it was blowing Force 6 to 7 from the south.

The two light cruisers, stationed well astern of the Battle Squadron, altered course towards the *Formidable*. The *Topaze* circled the ship and saw a dense cloud of smoke rise from the funnels as the second torpedo struck. Captain A N Loxley, commanding the *Formidable*, sent the *Topaze* for assistance to a single funnelled British steamer that was

Diamond's fore-gallant topmast, as well as her third cutter, were carried away as the ship rolled through 35 to 40 degrees.

Ordinary Seaman Walker, aged 18, was the youngest and last survivor to be picked up by the *Diamond*. When the *Formidable* was first torpedoed he was asleep in the fore lower messdeck. He was awakened by the explosion and hurried to the main mess deck where men were shouting to hurry up before the watertight doors were closed. Walker reached the upper deck and went to his station on the port side quarter deck. He noticed men busy moving all floatable objects. Two launches were lowered with great difficulty in the heavy seas and could not take their full complement of men, many of whom preferred in any case to stay on the ship.

After the second torpedo hit the battleship, Walker was by the rails on the quarter deck when the Engineer Commander next to him decided it was time to move. Walker slid down over the stern and landed in the water under one of the propellers. He kicked away from the suction of the sinking ship and grabbed hold of a floating object. He was in the water for two hours before being picked up by the *Diamond*. The seas were too rough

they were sent to rejoin their depot at Chatham.

Of the ship's complement of 780, 35 officers and 512 men of the *Formidable* were lost. Although the ship had remained afloat for more than two hours, the worsening weather and the winter cold must have caused the deaths of many, even though they may have escaped from the ship itself.

At 0800 1 January 1915 the remaining battleships entered Portland harbour and came to anchor. Vice Admiral Bayly prepared his report on the incident and forwarded it to the Secretary of the Admiralty. After a statement of the events of that fateful night, he

The cruiser HMS DIAMOND which, with her sister ship TOPAZE, brought survivors to Portland from the torpedoed battleship FORMIDABLE, January 1915.

AUTHOR'S COLLECTION

and he was too exhausted to catch the lifebelt thrown to him. It was only when an enterprising rescuer made a loop in a rope through which Walker could put his arm that he was hauled aboard.

Captain Loxley was last seen on the bridge of his ship. His dog, an Airedale called 'Bruce', was drowned and washed ashore on the Dorset coast below Abbotsbury Castle. Some of the ship's company got away in the cutter and, after twenty hours in the open boat, came ashore at Lyme Regis. Others were rescued from a waterlogged boat by superb seamanship on the part of the skipper of the Brixham trawler *Provident*.

The *Diamond* rejoined the fleet in Portland harbour and transferred her survivors to the battleship *Implacable*. After a day or two

concluded that he was justified in having his ships in single line. He recommended that all battleships should have auxiliary wireless (no wireless message was received from the *Formidable* after she had been struck), and that fishing boats should be kept at five miles distance from a Battle Squadron as they could act as a cover for a U-boat. He concluded by observing that no merchant ships had come to the *Formidable's* aid even though more than one was in sight.

Their Lordships at the Admiralty considerd Bayly's report and replied on 11 January:

> . . . from the track chart and signal logs forwarded by you, it would appear that you arrived off Portland harbour with your squadron at 4 am on 31st December and for a period of 24 hours remained between Portland and Start Point at a time when,

as you must have been fully aware, the English Channel was infested with enemy submarines.

The direct consequences of your prolonged stay in these dangerous waters was that the enemy's submarines were allowed ample opportunity to locate your squadron for the purpose of launching the successful attack made upon the *Formidable* at about 2.30 am on 1st January. With the evidence before them, My Lords can form no other conclusion than that the handling of your squadron for the period in question was marked by a want of prudence and good seamanship in avoidance of unnecessary risks inexplicable in an officer holding high and responsible command.

Their Lordships seemed unwilling to hear any explanation Bayly might have. Certainly there seemed to be no reason for him to think that the English Channel was 'infested' with enemy submarines. But his replies were not acceptable, his request for a court martial was denied, and he was told to haul down his flag on 17 January, to be relieved by Vice Admiral Bethell on the following day. Both Winston Churchill, the First Lord, and Admiral Fisher, the First Sea Lord, seemed determined to make an example of Bayly in drawing attention to the very real danger to capital ships presented by submarines armed with torpedoes. They supported the view that:

> More is demanded, and rightly demanded from those in high command than that they should shape their conduct of His Majesty's ships with such light hearted and stupid disregard for the dictates of prudence as revealed by this blunder.

Churchill realised that an Admiral could not always be held to be solely responsible for the loss of ships in wartime. After an appointment at Greenwich, Bayly was later appointed to the challenging post of Commander in Chief, Western Approaches, in which he gave distinguished service.

This serious loss certainly demonstrated the danger to major warships from the torpedo. Afterwards, whenever there was a threat from a suspected submarine in the area, most shipping movements came to a stop. On the very day that the *Formidable* was sunk, the battleship *Majestic* was on passage from Dover to Portland. On receipt of the news of the attack, she was ordered to enter Portsmouth, sailing again only at such time that she could make a night passage. She arrived at Portland and remained there until she sailed for the Dardanelles operation. Some risks had to be taken, however, and exercises continued. The new 15 inch gun battleship *Queen Elizabeth* carried out trials from Portland until she, too, at 0900 1 February 1915, sailed for the Mediterranean.

Shortly after the loss of HMS *Formidable*, additional precautions were taken to prevent U-boats entering Portland harbour. Orders were issued that two picket boats, each under the command of a commissioned officer, were to patrol outside the North entrance whenever the boom was opened in daylight. Each boat was to carry a 3 pdr gun and a charge of gun-cotton was placed in the stern sheets. Instructions were to ram a periscope if one was seen, to shoot at a conning tower and in any case to fire a gun and hoist a red burgee as a sign of danger. Vice Admiral Bethell was also concerned about security and loose talk about the movement of ships. He even went so far as to stop officers' leave for a time because they had talked too much while ashore.

A boom defence across the eastern entrance to Portland harbour, 1917. The chequered fort and its landing place are clearly visible.

Officers went ashore at Bincleaves, while ratings went to the Camber Jetty or Castletown Pier. Men were not to go more than four miles from their ships and were to keep a lookout for flags calling for their return.

Fighting the U-Boats

The threat of the U-boat was once more demonstrated in September 1916 when the 3rd Battle Squadron and two destroyer flotillas were at Portland. The Admiralty learned that a U-boat was operating between Beachy Head and Cap d'Antifer. All traffic was stopped though *Q 3*, a submarine decoy vessel once the cargo ship *Barranca* (4000 tons), sailed in anticipation of action. When fresh reports came in that a U-boat was at work off St Albans Head and another off Cap Barfleur, the British squadron was compelled to remain in harbour. Destroyers were sent out, not only from Portland but also from as far away as the Harwich Flotilla, until there were thirteen destroyers hunting U-boats in the Channel. It was not until activity died down that the battleships were risked at sea, several days after they were originally due to sail. The inefficient use of anti-submarine forces on such a large scale as this led to the formation of a centralised Anti-Submarine Division at the Admiralty.

More than sixty auxiliary vessels were by now operating from Portland and there were sufficient sightings and actions with German submarines to show that the enemy was using the English Channel as a patrol area and perhaps as a passage to the Atlantic. The number of occasions on which these auxiliaries picked up survivors of ships sunk by U-boats showed the increasing effectiveness of the German submarine war. On 14 September the trawler *Pelican II*, at sea with the trawler *Marconi* and the armed yacht *Lorna*, saw a large submarine with two periscopes surface close to a steamer. The steamer altered course, hoisted the signal that a submarine was in sight and blew her whistle. At this the U-boat moved away at high speed on the surface. In October 1916 the armed

yacht *Vanadis* saw a U-boat and in November the drifters *Sarepta* and *Sailor King* engaged a large submarine at close range 14 miles south west by south of Portland Bill.

The German submarine *UB 19* was sunk in the English Channel by the Q ship HMS *Penshurst* on 30 November 1916. The *Penshurst* had heard from ss *Ibex* of the presence of a submarine 20 miles WNW of the Casquets. Heading for this position she observed the conning tower of a U-boat that submerged as a seaplane flew over it. The aircraft, No. 8279, flown by Flight Sub Lieutenant J R Ross RN and AM W/T T J Redmond from Portland, alighted close to the *Penshurst* and plans were made for the ship and the aeroplane to co-operate in locating and attacking the German submarine. Unfortunately, the seaplane crashed on take-off, breaking a wing and floats, and began to sink. At this moment, as the crew were being brought aboard, *UB 19*, now on the surface, fired its first shots. The *Penshurst* carried out a prepared abandon ship procedure to make the enemy believe that this was simply a merchantman under attack. The U-boat drew closer and observed that the ship carried no name and was painted grey. The commander, Niemeyer, was immediately suspicious and ordered his boat to dive. At that moment the hidden guns aboard the *Penshurst* opened fire, shooting 83 rounds at the luckless submarine before she sank leaving 16 survivors to be picked up by the decoy ship.

In 1917 German submarine activity continued in the North Sea, the Atlantic and the Mediterranean. In the English Channel, frequent contacts were made with U-boats. Escort flotillas increased in number and though detection was sometimes by visual sighting, there was increasing use of hydrophones to detect the enemy under water. On 12 February the armed yacht *Vanessa* sighted a submarine at 6000 yards. She altered course and opened fire with her forward 6 pdr gun when she saw the submarine submerge. Continuing on her course the *Vanessa* sighted an oily patch but did not see any more of the U-boat. Later in the year an engagement took place between a U-boat and the trawler hydrophone flotilla under Lieutenant P Nicholson in the trawler *Maristo*. Shots were exchanged at 7000 yards as the submarine submerged. The periscope was observed later by the trawler *Caliph* close under her starboard bow. She turned and dropped a depth charge set at eighty feet, claiming a successful result, though no enemy submarine was reported as lost that day.

A number of skirmishes ended in this inconclusive way, neither side causing serious damage to the other, though the fact that the U-boat was forced to dive would cause it to travel more slowly, using precious power from the batteries that drove it while submerged. Immediate response to the sighting of the U-boat was imperative. This was made clear in a message from the Commodore, Portland, to all Motor Launch crews:

3 March 1917
Last night a submarine was sighted by a Motor Launch about 50 yards off and instead of the resolute action required, the CO proceeded to consult his consort thereby giving away to the submarine the presence of the ML and enabling her to dive.

Full speed at, or to cut off, the submarine immediately she was observed would probably have enabled the ML to use her depth charge, also the second ML would have been able to drop her depth charge as the MLs were close together.

I cannot emphasise too much the necessity for immediate action by the officer of the look-out, and also for having depth charges etc. constantly ready: in this case had the CO acted correctly the depth charge would have been required possibly a minute or less from sighting the submarine and going ahead. Dummy drill and rehearsal of sighting submarines should be practised in order to ensure that all details are remembered and carried out.

It was suggested that the officers who were to blame on this occasion should be cautioned.

U 85 made contact with the decoy vessel *Privet (Q 19)* off Start Point on 12 March 1917. Submerged, the submarine fired a single torpedo at the ship but missed. The U-boat commander, Petz, decided to surface and sink the small ship by gunfire. Hits were soon made on the *Privet* causing serious damage. The decoy vessel sent out an SOS but also revealed her true identity by opening fire on the German submarine, hitting the target four times before Petz could submerge. Though apparently trying to regain the surface, *U 85* was last seen sliding deeper into the sea stern first at an angle of 45 degrees. The *Privet* was so badly damaged in the encounter that she had to be towed to shallow water by a destroyer and allowed to sink to the bottom. She was, however, later raised and recommissioned.

The French Coal Trade

Portland was busy at this time patching up merchant ships, unloading trains with munitions and loading them into transports for the Western front. The Portland naval authorities were also responsible for the controlled sailings in the French coal trade. Some of the colliers had come under attack in the latter part of 1916 and the French requested some form of controlled sailings. There were three routes in this trade:

Route A   Mounts Bay to Brest
Route B: Weymouth to Cherbourg
Route C: Weymouth to Le Havre

The plan formulated required that colliers bound for Cherbourg and ports west, and colliers with speeds under eight knots bound for Brest and the Bay of Biscay ports should assemble at Portland. They were to leave in one group and time their arrival five miles north of Cherbourg at daylight. They would be met there by French patrols and piloted to their ports of destination. Times of sailing and routes were varied slightly by altering the point of departure from the English coast. If the ships were overtaken by fog or failed to rendezvous with the French patrols, they were to proceed independently. On moonlit nights, if the Senior Naval Officer Portland felt that there was a danger of submarine attack, then two armed trawlers were to be detailed to pilot the colliers across, remaining

Three short 830 seaplanes on the slip at Portland. In 1917 these machines flew anti-submarine patrols.

at Cherbourg until the next night when the homeward bound vessels would be piloted. The average daily crossing would be five small ships. The term 'pilotage' rather than 'convoy' was used for this trade. The ships hardly formed a convoy and they were not formally escorted. Instead they passed in company through patrolled waters. The resulting drop in casualties did, however, support the arguments for the establishment of a convoy system throughout the war zones.

Seaplanes v U-Boats

The threat of the German submarines brought the Royal Naval Air Service to Portland on active service. Having witnessed the first flight of an aircraft from a moving warship in 1912, the harbour now became a base from which seaplanes left on anti-submarine patrol. A hangar to accommodate the seaplanes was built between the Camber Jetty and the Loading Jetty, so allowing the seaplanes to use the existing target slipway when coming ashore. The air station was part of the Portsmouth group which established its headquarters at Calshot in 1917 and included another sub-station at Bembridge on the Isle of Wight. Additional stations were set up at Newhaven, Lee-on-Solent and Cherbourg for seaplanes, at Polegate for airships, and for balloons a station at Tipnor. During

1917 the air patrols encountered submarines on 27 occasions. They also provided a valuable service in locating the wreckage of ships sunk by U-boats, and in spotting survivors.

On 24 April Flight Lieutenant Scott attacked a U-boat 15 miles south of Portland Bill and dropped two bombs. On 15 May Sub-Lieutenant Ross, in aircraft 9846, spotted a periscope 20 miles south of Portland and dropped a 60lb bomb. A report on Ross's patrol well illustrates the work of the seaplanes:

At 1615 we received an urgent SOS signal from Q 19 saying that she had engaged a submarine and her engines were out of action. At 1630 Flight Sub Lieutenant Ross left the slipway but did not get off until 1650 owing to there being practically no wind. At 1735 he reached the required position but did not pick up the ship. Shortly afterwards he sighted two trawlers and turned eastwards over them. At 1750 he picked up a mass of wreckage and some oil. He then turned towards the trawlers and directed them to this position, afterwards carrying on his easterly course for about ten minutes then altering N30E. At 1820 he picked up more wreckage, two empty lifeboats and a large quantity of oil. At 1825 he sighted two more lifeboats with sails steering north east. He then returned to Portland and made full reports to the Commodore who was enabled to direct his searching parties to this position.

The last half hour of Ross's flight was in darkness. All the searchlights in the harbour were turned onto the water and a launch stood by in case he crash landed. At last his engine was heard, and after circling for five minutes to get his bearings, he made an excellent landing. This report clearly relates to the action between the *Privet (Q9)* and *U 85*.

The occupants of the two lifeboats were landed at Weymouth. They were from an Elder Dempster ship that had been torpedoed. The decoy ship was still afloat and was towed to port.

The technical difficulties of flying these early seaplanes is shown in a report by Flight Sub-Lieutenant Fox:

I left Portland on patrol 'X' in seaplane 8352 at 1115 on 1 February. My observer was AM W T Redman. At 1120 when off the Bill, the engine was vibrating so badly that the compass was almost useless, but I managed to steer a rough course by the sun. At 1220 I observed patches of oil on the water about five miles on my starboard side. At 1225 I was over the oil patches which were increasing in size, small bubbles rising to the surface and then spreading. At 1310 I steered south towards two French torpedo boats to warn them, firing two Very lights and signalling by lamp. The two torpedo boats were about six miles from the oil patches. At 1325 I returned to the oil but owing to the vibration I was obliged to throttle down the engine in order to get a bearing . . .

At 1440 I signalled a trawler with the lamp giving the position of the oil. She answered by running her answering pennant close up. I then steered for Portland against a strong wind. At 1630 I was forced to land owing to a leak in the oil system. The oil tank was found to be empty. At 1645 I was taken in tow by the trawler *Borneo* and arrived at Portland at 2230. The machine was undamaged except that the port wing float was lost.

Triumphs and Tragedies

A number of U-boats were sunk off Portland in the last two years of the war. *UC 62* struck a mine in October 1917 and was lost with all hands. *UC 51* was similarly lost off Start Point in November. In May 1918 two U-boats were destroyed, the first by the British submarine *D 4* and the second by the Portland based patrol vessel *Lorna*.

HMS *D 4 did* not come from Portland. She sailed from Portsmouth on 9 May, moored for a time alongside a depot ship in Yarmouth Roads before being escorted as far as Durleston Head. She reached her patrol area on Sunday 12 May and began the day lying stopped on the surface. At 0500 she dived to 20 feet and half an hour later sighted a German submarine proceeding on the surface

HMS HAZARD collided with the ambulance ship WESTERN AUSTRALIA and sank. WESTERN AUSTRALIA took survivors on-board.

at 6 knots. The British submarine made her attack 50 minutes after first sighting the U-boat. She fired two torpedoes and heard an explosion. Surfacing three minutes after the attack, she was able to rescue three seamen. There was no wreckage and no sign of any other survivors. The German submarine was *UB 72*, one of a group of U-boats attempting to make a concerted attack against troopships and the newly introduced convoys. *D4* reported the position of the sunken U-boat as 50.05N, 02.41W, south of Lyme Bay.

Exactly two weeks later, 26 May, the armed yacht *Lorna* attacked *UB 74*, again in Lyme Bay. The U-boat was heading for operations off St Nazaire when she was sighted at a distance of 50 yards. Sweeping in to attack, the *Lorna* scraped the submarine's conning tower. She passed over the top and dropped two depth charges set at 50 feet. As they exploded the *Lorna* turned in a tight circle to attack again and at that moment four men came to the surface amongst bubbles of air, gas and oil. Not appreciating that *UB 74* was already mortally stricken, a third depth charge was dropped. Unfortunately the explosion killed three of the men in the water and so injured the fourth that he died after being taken aboard the British ship. The loss of *UB 74* was confirmed on 30 May when the wreck was located by trawlers using chain ground sweeps. The next day divers found the submarine. The mark of the *Lorna's* stem was visible on the port side abaft the conning tower. Damage 40 feet long and three inches wide was found under the saddle tank on the port side extending from abreast the conning tower.

Two tragic collisions occurred during the early months of 1918. HMS *Hazard*, employed as a submarine depot ship, was in collision with the ambulance ship *Western Australia* on 28 January. The *Hazard* was sunk but a number of the ship's company were saved, being taken aboard *Western Australia*. Ironically, *Hazard* had assisted in the rescue of survivors from another hospital ship, ss *Anglia*, when she struck a mine off Folkestone in 1915.

Perhaps more tragic still was the loss of the destroyer *Bittern* off Portland in thick fog on the early morning of 4 April. She was struck by ss *Kenilworth*. The destroyer was overwhelmed and sank quickly with the loss of all hands. A Court of Inquiry found negligence on the part of the master of ss *Kenilworth*. His instructions had been to hug the coast as closely as possible from Portland Bill to Start Point. Instead he headed straight across, showing no lights nor sounding for fog. At 0315 the *Kenilworth* saw a red light and a ship 'small and low down' at the moment of impact. The *Bittern* must have gone down like a stone.

The low profile of HMS BITTERN made her almost invisible in fog to the steamer KENILWORTH.

5

BETWEEN THE WARS

Post-War Economies and the Home Fleet

In the years after the war, British interests at home and across the world had to be maintained. At sea there was no obvious enemy against whom to prepare. Naval rivalries certainly existed, not only with European powers, but also with Japan and the United States of America. The Overseas and Home Ports Defence Committee considered forms and scales of attack on British ports, including Portland. Such forms were identified as:- by raider, gunfire and minelaying; by cruisers, destroyers, coastal motor boats and boom smashers; by mine and torpedo attacks on shipping in the approaches to the port; and by raiding parties landed from warships or merchant vessels. Potential enemies, as identified in 1922, were France, Italy, Japan and the USA. Of these it was considered that Italy and Japan would not be able to threaten Portland. The United States navy, however, could attack the harbour and its shipping by minelaying and by gunfire from raiding vessels, while France, the 'old enemy', could mount all the listed forms of attack.

There was also the threat from the air, though there is little evidence that its possible effect on Portland was then foreseen. In an exercise soon after the war, the Second Battle Squadron of the Atlantic Fleet was attacked while at anchor in Portland harbour by torpedo carrying aircraft. Unable to dodge the practice torpedoes, the ships were sitting ducks and it was claimed that seven out of the eight torpedoes dropped had hit their targets. This may well have been the first occasion that a fleet was attacked while at its base. Admiral Sir Charles Madden observed that, even at its present stage of development, the torpedo plane was the most dangerous form of torpedo attack upon heavy ships.

The war left Britain beset by economic and financial difficulties. For the Royal Navy, contraction following the massive expansion of the wartime fleet meant that every aspect of expenditure was closely examined. The reaction against war also meant that international agreements were sought to reduce and limit armaments. There was even a strong lobby in Britain for the abolition of the submarine as a weapon of war. Although not implemented, such a policy would have had serious implications for those branches of the navy dealing with anti-submarine work, much of which would be carried out at Portland.

The Grand Fleet was abolished in 1919 and Admiral Sir David Beatty hauled down his flag. An Atlantic Fleet was formed under Admiral Sir Charles Madden with nine battleships and five battle cruisers supported by two aircraft carriers and numbers of cruisers, destroyers and submarines. A second fleet, called the Home Fleet, under Admiral Sir Henry Oliver, had a short life. It was established, reduced to reserve and then abolished all within a year. The abolition was in the interests of economy and the six battleships and six cruisers were retained in reserve with reduced complement. Occasional test mobilisation gave the ships opportunities for exercising at sea. Rear Admiral Sir Douglas Nicholson was appointed Rear Admiral Reserve Fleet with his headquarters at Portland, but on completion of his term, he was succeeded, as Senior Officer Reserve Fleet Portland, by an officer of Captain's rank.

The desire to economise threatened the facilities at Portland. Even though it was recognised that the base was favourably placed for submarine and anti-submarine exercises, nevertheless a committee recommended that the yard be closed, that ships should be transferred to Portsmouth and that only the provision of oil fuel should remain. This potentially disastrous situation for the base was partly relieved by Sir David Beatty, then First Sea Lord, who complained that the papers on this matter had only come to his attention by a fortunate accident. Though he was in favour of economies wherever possible, he supported the continuation of anti-submarine work at Portland. A Board of Admiralty minute of 21 December 1922 stated that the maintenance of Portland was important as:

a. the southern rendezvous in home waters of the Atlantic Fleet.
b. it possesses large fuel installations which are being extended, and a well equipped coaling depot.

cluded that it was most desirable that Portland be retained as an up-to-date naval base. This view was supported by the Director of Plans, Captain (later Admiral of the Fleet and First Sea Lord) Dudley Pound, who stated in May 1923:

Portland, as far as can be foreseen, will on occasion be required as a naval anchorage for capital ships in a war with a northern European power.

It is interesting to note that, in a memo on the status of the base, the Commander in Chief, Portsmouth, noted that the only disadvantage of Portland was that "it was too open to air attack in war to be ideally suitable." In the light of events nearly twenty years later, this was a prophetic observation.

The continuation of Portland's active in-

HMS VULCAN was launched in 1889 as a torpedo boat carrier. At Portland in the early 1920s she served as depot ship to the submarine periscope school.

The work of the base also involved considerable handling of stores, transit to ships, maintenance of stores for immediate requirements, and the maintenance of refuelling craft afloat, as well as pumping and coaling machinery ashore. Admiral J M de Robeck, Commander in Chief, Atlantic Fleet, argued for the retention of most of these facilities, stating that the importance of Portland as a naval base had been enhanced since the termination of the war with Germany. He con-

volvement with the Royal Navy was confirmed by the decision, on 11 December 1923, that the base be known henceforth as 'HM Naval Base, Portland'. It was then possible for those activities that had engaged the base for many years to be maintained and extended.

It was about this time that correspondence took place on the possibility of Cunard liners using Portland as a port of embarkation for Atlantic passengers. Sir Aubrey Brockle-

The early 1920s.
The destroyer pens are occupied by H class submarines and 'P' and 'PC' class patrol boats. The battle cruiser HOOD is in the harbour with a battleship, several 'V & W' class destroyers, depot ships, merchant vessels and coal hulks.

bank, Chairman of Cunard, first wrote to the Admiralty in 1923, indicating that four liners might be used. The Admiralty discussed the proposals and raised no material objections provided that the naval establishments were not seriously affected. Although one battleship buoy would be lost and others moved to clear a channel for the liners, and the coaling pier would have to be extended, it

Discipline was very strict with precise regulations for punishment, including 'cuts' with the cane. Boy seamen were out scrubbing decks at 0530, even in snow and ice. They received very little pay, not enough even to enable them to get by train or bus into Weymouth. They were often to be found walking round Portland with very little else to do. Boy seamen were not required,

The Battleship COLOSSUS, one of the Battleships that served as Boys Training ships.

AUTHOR'S COLLECTION

was felt that the advantages, particularly to the general benefit of employment in the area, would outweight the disadvantages. The plan, however, seems not to have been pursued further.

The Anti-Submarine Flotilla had already been established at Portland in HMS *Gibraltar* in 1922, while The Periscope School was in HMS *Vulcan*. The Boys' Training Establishment was set up on 22 September 1921 with the commissioning of the battleships *Colossus* and *Collingwood*. Cadets still endured at least some of the rigours of their predecessors in HMS *Boscawen*. Some duties were carried out in bare feet and each lad slept in a nightshirt 'cadets for the use of'.

however, to stand night watches. The *Collingwood* was withdrawn and paid off in March 1922, and the *Colossus* left Portland for Devonport on 11 May 1922, having transferred the remaining boys to other establishments. As well as the cadets' training ships the gunnery firing ship *Orion* was also at Portland and there were usually about seven submarines there in reserve. The Atlantic Fleet and its attendant destroyers were in the harbour for as much as six or seven months of the year.

The three-funnelled battle-cruiser *Tiger* was at Portland as seagoing gunnery firing ship from 1924 to 1929. In a typical period from 1927 to 1928 she sailed with the battle-

The battlecruiser TIGER fought at Dogger Bank and Jutland in the First World War. She was a seagoing gunnery training ship at Portland from 1924 to 1929.

ships *Nelson*, *Revenge* and *Iron Duke* for 6 inch and 6 pdr gunnery practice. In the spring of 1928 she sailed with HMS *Nelson*, *Rodney*, *Iron Duke*, *Benbow*, *Emperor of India*, *Marlborough*, *Hood*, *Repulse* and *Renown*, while cruisers of the 2nd Cruiser Squadron and destroyers of the 6th Flotilla escorted the capital ships. On 3rd April the King of Afghanistan visited Portland. Prince George was serving aboard *Nelson* at the time and went ashore accompanied by Lieutenant Commander E Pleydell-Bouverie to meet the King. The ship's company of HMS *Tiger* formed the guard of honour when the King's railway Pullman coach was brought opposite the Camber Jetty. Rain and mist prevented the whole of the planned programme from taking place, but the *Nelson*, the *Rodney*, ships of the 3rd Battle Squadron, the battle cruisers *Renown* and *Repulse*, the aircraft carrier HMS *Furious*, cruisers and destroyers passed before the visitor. The four destroyers of the Anti-Submarine Flotilla, *Thruster*, *Salmon*, *Torrid* and *Rowena* sailed past at speed. While the *Tiger* and other ships remained at Portland, the *Nelson*, with the King of Afghanistan aboard sailed on to Spithead. Later in the month the *Tiger* carried out a bombardment exercise in West Bay off Abbotsbury, no doubt vibrating and even shattering windows ashore.

The fire of the battleships' guns sometimes caused windows to be broken in houses close to Chesil Beach, and residents learned the wisdom of keeping their windows open when firing was in progress. It was even rumoured that shock waves from the 16 inch guns of the *Nelson* and *Rodney* had brought down chimney pots on Portland.

On 29 May the *Tiger* went to the assistance of a private aircraft that had crashed in Weymouth Bay close to the Dutch liner *Ryndan*. The battle cruiser's pinnace raced to the scene. Though the pilot was already dead, the mechanic was rescued with cuts and bruises.

The flagship *Nelson* was once more in Portland harbour in October 1935 with Admiral Sir Roger Backhouse as Commander-in-Chief. The ship had on board a prototype amphibian aircraft, a Supermarine Walrus. A large crane on the port side of the battleship hoisted the aircraft into the water before take off and recovered it after landing. On 5 October the pilot Lieutenant J de F Jago and his observer Lieutenant Comander A D Torlesse prepared to take the Commander in Chief to London for a conference at the Admiralty. The aircraft, K 4797, took off from the harbour and flew to Hendon where its wheels were lowered to enable it to land at Hendon airfield. On the return journey in the afternoon, again with the Admiral on board, low cloud kept the Walrus below 2000 feet. At that height the wheels were not retracted while the machine was over land. Approaching Portland the weather cleared and Lieutenant Jago brought his aircraft down to alight close to the flagship. Unfortunately, with the wheels still in the lowered position, the machine crashed as it hit the water. The three men on board were quickly rescued, none apparently seriously injured, but all with minor cuts. Sir Roger Backhouse, 6 feet 4 inches tall, cannot have found escape easy and he was badly shaken. He refused to take the rest necessary to aid his recovery and it is very likely that the crash contributed to his giving up the post of First Sea Lord to which he was appointed in November 1938. He died on 15 July 1939.

The log of the battleship recorded that the Walrus was hoisted aboard at 1835. After repair it returned to the fleet for further service, though not aboard the *Nelson*. As a result of the accident klaxon horns were fitted to Walrus aircraft to give the pilot warning that the undercarriage was down.

Asdic, Anti-Submarine Warfare and HMS Osprey

As early as 1917, Captain W Fisher, Director of the Anti-Submarine Division at the Admiralty, had suggested that an anti-submarine establishment should be built at Portland on the site of the rifle range there. The Admiralty works representative visited Portland in August that year. As a result, approval was given for the expenditure of £5,000 on buildings and £5,000 on fitting out the workshops. In the meantime anti-submarine training was urgently needed and temporary accommodation was provided at Portland and commissioned as HMS *Sarepta*. Sea instruction was given in the trawler *Companion* and drifter *Phyllis Mary*. Experimental work was carried out in the sheds on the inner breakwater, and the dockyard swimming pool was used for testing towed 'Fish' hydrophones. When new buildings were completed in April 1918 it was possible to provide training for two hundred officers and men.

On 11 November 1918 the Armistice ended hostilities with Germany. In December Captain Humphrey Walwyn RN arrived at Portland in HMS *Gibraltar* to start the task of demobilising the auxiliary patrol vessels. Some two hundred trawlers, many fitted with hydrophones, lay three or four abreast, right across the harbour. However, a year after the *Gibraltar's* arrival, the work of the anti-submarine school was transferred to her and *Sarepta* closed down. Successful trials of experimental Asdic sets were carried out soon afterwards. The anti-submarine school was then opened once more, still as HMS *Sarepta*. The objects of the school were:

a. to instruct officers and ratings sent to the school prior to them joining ships fitted with hydrophones.

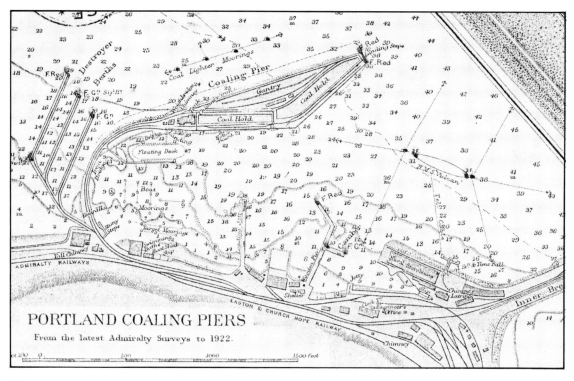

PORTLAND COALING PIERS

From the latest Admiralty Surveys to 1922.

b. to carry out experiments ashore to improve the hydrophones.

c. to carry out sea experiments in co-operation with the Admiralty research laboratories, combined with sea instruction of the personnel concerned.

The staff of the school consisted of five officers and fifty ratings.

As part of the task of reducing expenditure, the Admiralty had considered the feasibility of reducing dockyard services at Portland. However, the First Lord's statement with the estimates for 1920/21 acknowledged that regard must be paid to the efficient maintenance of the anti-submarine organisation.

> Another branch of the service that did not exist when the war began is the Anti-submarine school; the importance of this school in the future can hardly be over-estimated. We have seen the great effort which was made by means of the submarine to wrest from us our sea supremacy. Science alone can give us the antidote to the submarine, and we have taken steps, as will be seen in the detailed statement regarding the fleet, to ensure progress in experimental work and training. Development in this work will undoubtedly be required to meet the possibilities of the future, and proposals are under consideration for the establishment of a school of anti-submarine work in conjunction with the anti-submarine experimental station.

In the following year, the First Lord identified this anti-submarine work in detail:

> The importance of the research work in connection with the anti-submarine devices has been kept in continuous review, as progress in this direction must have a profound effect in regard to the requirements of design and types of vessels in the future. The anti-submarine school has been set up in the existing buildings at Portland, and already there is considerable promise for the future in certain detection devices under trial. Three vessels attached to the school at Portland are specially fitted for the practical experiments which are being pursued, the officers carrying out these trials being in close touch with the Scientific Establishments concerned, thus ensuring that the theoretical requirements receive due weight.

In 1923 the *Gibraltar* paid off and was replaced by HMS *Heather*, a sloop built in 1916. A more permanent move was made in the following year when on 1 April 1924, HMS *Osprey* was commissioned as the anti-submarine school. It was an independent command which acted as parent ship to the First Anti-submarine Flotilla. Captain S D

HMS GIBRALTAR was completed in 1894 as a first class protected cruiser. In 1919, having no fighting value, she came to Portland as a depot ship.

Tillard was appointed as Captain of HMS *Osprey*. He was a survivor of the sinking of the cruiser *Hogue* by a U-boat in 1914 and had served in the battleship *Barham* at the Battle of Jutland. He later set up his headquarters ashore in 1927.

Captain S D Tillard was the first captain of HMS OSPREY in 1924.

Within six months of the establishment of the Osprey, Captain Tillard expressed to the Admiralty his criticism of the effectiveness of the widely scattered research and development establishments involved in anti-sub-

marine work, and argued for a single establishment to be set up at Portland. He also wished to see a close link between research and development and the anti-submarine school. His proposal received strong support from the Admiralty. Following reports by a committee under Rear Admiral W E Napier, it was proposed that the Captain of the Anti-submarine school should be in control of all staff, civilian and service alike, engaged in experimental work. This centralisation of resources was approved and led to the appointment of B S Smith as Chief Scientist at HMS *Osprey* in 1927.

The period that followed, leading up to the outbreak of war again in 1939, was devoted to the development and assembly of devices to detect, track and kill submarines. Such devices, preferably presenting information directly to those on the bridge, had to operate effectively with the attacking warship moving at speed.

In the early 1920s, the anti-submarine flotilla based at Portland consisted of HM Patrol Vessels *P 31*, *P 38*, *P 40*, *PC 73* and *PC 74*, with *P 59* as a trials ship. In addition the whalecatchers *Icewhale* and *Cachalot* were fitted with Asdic sets in the same year. The P boats, however, were found to be unsuitable for Asdic as their draught was too shallow. HMS *Heather* was also inadequate because her speed was too slow to enable her to keep

CROWN COPYRIGHT

WRIGHT & LOGAN

HMS HEATHER replaced the GIBRALTAR at Portland in 1923. A sloop, she was built to look like a merchant man and so attract enemy submarines.

HMS P 40 was part of the Anti-Submarine Flotilla at Portland in the early 1920s. She displaced only 613 tons and could reach 23 knots when new.

up with other ships during exercises. In 1925, therefore, these older ships were replaced by the destroyers *Rowena, Salmon, Thruster* and *Torrid.* The flotilla went to sea on three or four days a week, taking out classes of operators from the anti-submarine school, exercising with submarines and sometimes taking part in larger exercises screening an imaginary fleet in the English Channel. A steady improvement in anti-submarine exercises was marked by the retention of contact with submarines over longer periods and under adverse weather conditions that would once have caused loss of contact. It was found

that operating Asdic successfully was an art rather than a science. A sensitive operator could distinguish between rocks, shoals of fish, wrecks and submarines.

A letter of appreciation to those engaged in anti-submarine training was proposed in March 1926. It was to be sent to all those concerned, but the Admiralty felt that congratulatory messages had become too commonplace during the war, and should now only be sent on occasions when the normal high and exacting standards had been surpassed. A verbal message of congratulation was eventually sent to Captain Tillard who then in-

HMS PC 74 served with the anti-submarine flotilla for a period between the wars and acted as a decoy ship in the first month of World War II. She also managed to sink the coal hulk HAYTIAN in Portland harbour in February 1937 having developed steering trouble while shifting berths.

WRIGHT & LOGAN

Ships of the anti-submarine flotilla sail from Portland on exercise, with ROWENA and SALMON nearest the camera. 1925.

formed all those under his command.

The first Asdic fitted to a submarine was installed in *H 32* in 1922, to be followed by several L class vessels. Work went ahead for the development of Asdics for trawlers as well as destroyers and sloops. Sets designed for the detection of submarines and torpedoes were fitted to battleships and cruisers. Sea trials of an early course plotter were carried out in the battle cruiser *Hood* in 1925 and later sets were fitted to the battleships *Nelson, Rodney* and *Revenge* as well as the cruisers *Norfolk, Devonshire* and *Berwick*. Personnel from the *Osprey* were concerned with the development of an Admiralty echo sounder. Newly designed sloops for ocean escort, later to become the Black Swan class, and coastal escorts of the Kingfisher class were fitted with Asdic sets, as were all destroyers after 1932. Work on forward throwing weapons was begun, then stopped, only to be resumed just before the war began. Although given low priority, static harbour defence by Asdic reached the stage of sea trials at Portland in 1932 when a submarine was detected at a distance of 2000 yards.

Asdic research and training remained shrouded in secrecy and the Admiralty went to great lengths to keep it so. Some of those with knowledge of the work going on rated the achievements of Asdic more highly than

they deserved, for in fact the success rates were relatively low and there were many false contacts. Trials showed that success could more likely be achieved by the use of a second vessel to direct the attacking ship onto the target submarine. It was to prove fortunate for the Royal Navy that some service personnel committed themselves and their careers to anti-submarine warfare. The branch was not a popular choice for ambitious officers between the wars, but among those who did devote their service careers to defence against the submarine were Commander (later Captain) F J Walker and Commander (later Rear Admiral) C D Howard Johnston. Success against the U-boats in 1939-45 depended much upon the skill and training of these men and those who learned from them.

The training programme at the anti-submarine school was at first to train the few hydrophone operators still on active service in the use of Asdic. There would be two levels of achievement. Some ratings would become qualified to take charge of Asdic sets while others would be operators pure and simple. As it became clear that more men were required, volunteers were called for from appropriate branches of the Atlantic Fleet. By 1928 the flow of volunteers was again insufficient, so the whole branch was reorganised and volunteers for Submarine Detection

Operators were drawn from trained men. A distinguishing badge was introduced in 1930 and the permanence of the branch was thus visibly established.

By 1938 the policy was to train sufficient ratings to meet requirements if the international situation required the mobilisation of the navy. It was hoped to reach a figure of more than 1300 trained operators by the middle of 1940, and to achieve this instructors at the school would have to work at full stretch. In submarines, every wireless rating joining the branch from 1938 had to qualify as a Telegraphist Detector at HMS *Osprey*. Those already in the branch were sent to qualify as opportunity occurred.

Ratings qualifying as Submarine Detection Operators could not be more than 25 years of age when they joined the *Osprey* and they had to have been assessed as satisfactory or above for ability. They had to have full normal hearing and must not suffer from excessive seasickness as much of their sea time would be spent in small ships.

In June 1938, Winston Churchill, accompanied by the First Sea Lord, visited Portland to see Asdic at work. Churchill went to sea in a destroyer and watched another destroyer guide his ship onto its target. Writing later in his history of the Second World War, Churchill acknowledged that he may at the time have overrated the level of success achieved. Nevertheless, he recognised the value of the work of all concerned, and declared that even though Asdics were not able to conquer the U-boats on their own, without them the U-boat could not have been conquered at all.

As Germany began once more to build submarines, the Committee of Imperial Defence considered the potential danger to British trade should war break out again. In October 1938, the Admiralty view was:

> Should Germany make vigorous use of her available submarine forces, our counter measures should enable us to prevent her from obtaining a marked success even by unrestricted warfare, although we must expect losses in the initial stages.

Four months later, perhaps already aware that war was imminent, that the Royal Navy possessed fewer than half the escorts it required to protect convoys and that air cover would be less than adequate, there was less optimism:

> Germany's submarine forces, though limited, might well do serious damage in the Western Approaches and the narrow seas, particularly if linked with aircraft.

The importance of the anti-submarine work conducted at Portland between the wars cannot be overestimated. Though it can be argued that insufficient attention was given in fleet exercises to the protection of trade against submarines, at least the work was begun that eventually brought about the defeat of the U-boats in the later stages of the war. It was, however, a close run thing.

Apart from the threat of the submarine, the Admiralty was also concerned with the protection of ships against new types of torpedoes and mines. An Anti-non-Contact Committee was set up in 1936 responsible for the investigation of problems in devising counter measures to torpedoes operated by magnetic pistols as well as the threat posed by magnetic mines. Experiments centred upon a cable carrying electric current which girded the ship horizontally. The cruiser *Curacoa* and the old battleship *Iron Duke* were chosen for experiments on magnetisation. At trials held at Portland in 1938, the coil set off the magnetic pistol of an approaching torpedo at a safe range from the target ship.

Submarine Incidents in Portland Waters Between the Wars

Submarine and anti-submarine training meant that submarines were frequently present at Portland. From the base they worked with the fleet, carrying out attacks on capital ships and exercising with destroyers in developing anti-submarine techniques. Over the years this led to a number of incidents, some of them tragic, particularly when the submerged submarines and surface ships were in close proximity.

In March 1920 the submarine *H 51* surfaced close to the destroyer *Warwick*. The submarine's commander was accused of hazarding his ship, even though no collision occurred. In January 1924, the submarine *L 24* was less fortunate.

An exercise was planned to start on 10 January. Its aim was to exercise submarines in receiving reports from aircraft and in attacking a battle fleet. The 'Blue' fleet consisted of the depot ship *Maidstone*, the minesweeper *Ross* and five groups of submarines:

No 1: *L 24*(SO), *H 23*, *H 48*
No 2: *L 25*, *H 31*, *H 27*
No 3: *H 22*, *H 24*
No 4: *H 30*, *H 29*
No 5: *H 52*, *H 34*

The 'Red' fleet included the battleship *Queen Elizabeth*, the 1st Battle Squadron, the 2nd Light Cruiser Squadron, the cruiser *Coventry* and the 1st, 2nd and 5th Destroyer Flotillas, the minelayer *Princess Margaret* and the destroyer *Telemachus*. The 'Blue' fleet submarines were to be in position by 0800 10 January.

HMS *Resolution*, a battleship of the 1st Battle Squadron, left Portland with the squadron and reached a position nearly ten miles from Portland Bill at 1113. The submarine *L 24*, with her group, had already sailed at 0355, dived at 0930 and prepared to attack the battle fleet. The battleships were proceeding at 11 knots when a periscope was sighted close to the *Resolution's* port bow. The periscope was seen from the battleship next ahead, the *Revenge*. The *Resolution* felt a slight bump and her paravane chain parted at a depth of 32 feet. Captain J E T Harper of the *Resolution* described the sea conditions as:-

> sea calm, no white horses about, but a slight swell to which the ship was rising and falling sufficiently for a small amount of spray to come over the stem and come up the hawse pipe on two or three occasions after passing Portland Bill.

It seemed that *L 24*, having penetrated the destroyer screen, tried to pass between the *Resolution* and the *Revenge*, had to dive to get clear, but was struck by the stem of the *Resolution* coming down on the fall. She was

One of the notoriously unlucky K class of submarines . . . K22 was stranded on the Portland breakwater in 1924.

forced downwards and struck again by the hull of the battleship. Lieutenant Commander Paul L Eddis, four other commissioned officers, one warrant officer and thirty five ratings lost their lives. There were no survivors and the submarine came to rest some 10 miles south of Portland Bill in 30 fathoms.

Later the same year, the steam driven submarine *K 22*, sailing at night in company with her sister ship *K 2*, the light cruiser *Conquest* and the minesweeper *Fermoy*, passed on the wrong side of a floating light on the north side of the entrance to Portland harbour and became stranded on the breakwater until she was towed off by the cruiser *Frobisher*. The commanding officer and navigating officer of *K 22* were severely reprimanded.

The year 1925 saw its share of continuing submarine disasters when the *M 1* was lost off Start Point. She had sailed with her sister ship *M 3* and both had dived together. The *M 1* was not heard of again, though the merchantman ss *Vidar* struck a submerged object off Start Point at about the time that *M 1* would have been in the area. Surface warships and submarines from Portland searched the area, but there were no survivors. In a memorial service conducted at sea three lines of ships sailed at four knots in a choppy sea over the spot where the missing submarine might be, wallowing and rolling as the service was held.

A tragedy similar to that which befell the *L 24* was narrowly averted when, in March 1928, the submarine *R 4*, coming to the surface from a dive of 40 feet, rose beneath the destroyer *Thruster* and struck her. Both the submarine's periscopes were smashed or bent. Fortunately she returned safely to moor alongside the depot ship *Vulcan* at Portland.

The strangest event was that concerning the submarine *M 2* in January 1932. The *M 2* was an unconventional submarine. She was laid down in 1918 as the *K 19*, one of the steam driven boats designed to work with the Grand Fleet. Her surface displacement was 1600 tons and she was 303 feet long. She was completed, however, not as the *K 19*, but as

the *M 2*, one of a class of three monitor submarines with diesel instead of steam engines and mounting a 12 inch gun forward of the conning tower. In 1927 the gun was removed and in its place an aircraft hangar was built for a small seaplane. The Parnall Peto was designed to fly from the *M 2*. It was built of stainless steel, had a wing span of 28 ft 5 in (8 feet with folded wings) and could be catapulted from the deck of the submarine.

The morning of 26 January 1932 was calm with sea fog patches. The submarine *M 2* was exercising in West Bay. At 1011 she signalled to her depot ship *Titania* at Portland: 'About to commence exercises.' No further signal was received from her. By late afternoon there was increasing anxiety at Portland that something was wrong with the submarine. At 1700 two other submarines left harbour to begin a search. Sailors ashore were recalled, announcements being made in cinemas and the theatre. At 2020 four destroyers set out. Within a short time a number of other ships, including the depot ship *Adamant* and local minesweeping and anti-submarine flotillas were at sea trying to locate the missing *M 2*. At last a naval seaplane spotted a patch of oil in West Bay and directed HM Trawler *Blackwater* to the area. This vessel located the wreck by use of her hydrophone. In that part of West Bay, however, the sea bottom was littered with wrecks and it was not until 3 February that a searching vessel could signal:

Have located submarine *M 2* in position approximately 312 degrees 5.8 miles Portland Bill.

The following day another signal reported:

First examination of forepart shows ship with a small list to starboard. Hangar door wide open. Aeroplane and rail gauge in hangar. Fore hatch closed.

Later reports showed that the upper conning tower hatch was open, but the engine room hatch was closed. During the search the body of a leading seaman was recovered and identified.

It seemed at first that the cause of the loss of *M 2* would never be known. But then someone remembered the casual remark of a mer-

The aircraft carrying submarine M2, later lost with all hands.

chant skipper at Portland who was understood to have talked of the abnormal behaviour of a naval vessel. By the time the comment was reported the skipper and his ship, ss *Tynesider*, had sailed. She was located however at Gravelines and the destroyer *Scimitar* was despatched to get a statement from him. A minor international incident was created by the *Scimitar* entering Belgian territorial waters apparently without prior permission. The evidence from members of the crew of the *Tynesider* was that some of them had been watching a submarine and had the impression that she dived stern first, with the bows lifting from the water as the boat went down. The merchant captain thought this was unusual but considered the foggy conditions may have given a false impression

of what really occurred. This vital evidence, linked with the discoveries of the divers who examined the wreck, seemed to show that, on surfacing, the hangar door had been opened prematurely, with the result that the submarine was flooded and slid back beneath the waves.

The event received considerable publicity and the Admiralty issued many details to the press, at the same time being anxious that no mention should be made of Asdic, which had been of considerable value in the search for and discovery of *M 2*. Attempts to raise the ship eventually failed and the wreck became a target for anti-submarine Asdic exercises.

An incident involving a German submarine was reported in the summer of 1937. Answering a question in the House of Commons, the

The destroyer HMS SCIMITAR was sent to collect eye witness accounts of the sinking of the submarine M2 in West Bay in 1932. She was damaged by air attack in Portland Harbour in August 1940. Accidental damage in 1944 prevented her from joining the ill fated convoy of US landing craft in exercises off South Devon.

First Lord of the Admiralty, Duff Cooper, reported that there had been a U-boat in territorial waters off Portland Bill on 21 July 1937. British destroyers and a submarine were exercising in the area. The destroyer *Walpole* first sighted the U-boat and sig-nalled the submarine *Spearfish* to come to the surface. *Walpole* and *Wolfhound* observed that the German vessel had the number *34* on the conning tower. By strange coincidence it was *U 34* that torpedoed the *Spearfish* off Norway on 1 August 1940.

Fleet Reviews

The wide expanse of Weymouth Bay, adjacent to the harbour and naval base at Portland, provided an admirable setting for reviews of the fleet. Though Spithead had traditionally been the location of Jubilee and Coronation Reviews, Weymouth too, had witnessed the assembly of ships, either for a full review or as a rendezvous point before proceeding elsewhere for a formal occasion.

The reviews of 1912 and 1914 have already been mentioned. Between the wars, the King reviewed his fleet at Weymouth on several occasions. The Atlantic Fleet, commanded by Admiral Sir Henry Oliver paid an official visit to Weymouth in July 1927 for ten days. His flagship HMS *Revenge*, was accompanied by the battleships *Ramillies, Iron Duke, Emperor of India, Benbow* and *Marlborough*, the battle cruisers *Hood* and *Repulse* and the aircraft carrier *Furious*. The new minelaying cruiser *Adventure* accompanied the older HMS *Centaur* and the fleet was completed by the 2nd Cruiser Squadron, the 5th and 6th Destroyer Flotillas and ships of the Fleet Target Service. A programme of receptions and entertainments organised for officers and men, and ships were open to visitors on each day of the visit. The Navy organised several pulling regattas among the squadrons of the fleet, and there was a Midshipman's gig race and sailing race. Ashore there was a tennis tournament, a concert by the massed bands of the fleet and a Reception and Ball at the Royal Palm Court. Sailors in uniform were admitted free to the Athletic Sports meeting held at the Recreation Ground.

Five years later, King George V, accompanied by the Prince of Wales and Prince George arrived in the Royal Yacht *Victoria and Albert* escorted by destroyers *Windsor* and *Westminster*. The First Lord of the Admiralty, Sir Bolton Eyres-Monsell was also present to review the ships of the recently designated Home Fleet under Admiral Sir John Kelly. His flagship was the battleship *Nelson*. Astern of her lay the Royal Yacht, the battleship *Warspite* and the eight inch gun cruiser *Dorsetshire*. A second line was composed of the *Rodney, Hood, Malaya* and *Norfolk*, and a third line of the aircraft carrier HMS *Courageous*, the battle cruiser *Renown*, the battleship *Valiant* and the cruiser *Exeter*. The aircraft carrier *Furious* was also present and 27 destroyers were assembled in their flotillas.

Following the death of the 'Sailor King', George V, the uncrowned Edward VIII visited the fleet in November 1936 before his abdication. He was popular in the navy and enjoyed a smoking concert in HMS *Courageous*. King George VI was crowned on 12 May 1937. The Coronation Review of the Fleet began a week later at Spithead. The new king had had a naval training, being appointed to the battleship *Collingwood* in 1913. He served aboard her during the Battle of Jutland and later joined the battleship *Malaya*.

In July 1938 the King visited the Home Fleet at Weymouth. He was accompanied by his brother the Duke of Kent, the Right Hon A Duff Cooper, First Lord of the Admiralty, and Admiral Sir A Ernle M Chatfield, First Sea Lord. The Commander-in-Chief of the

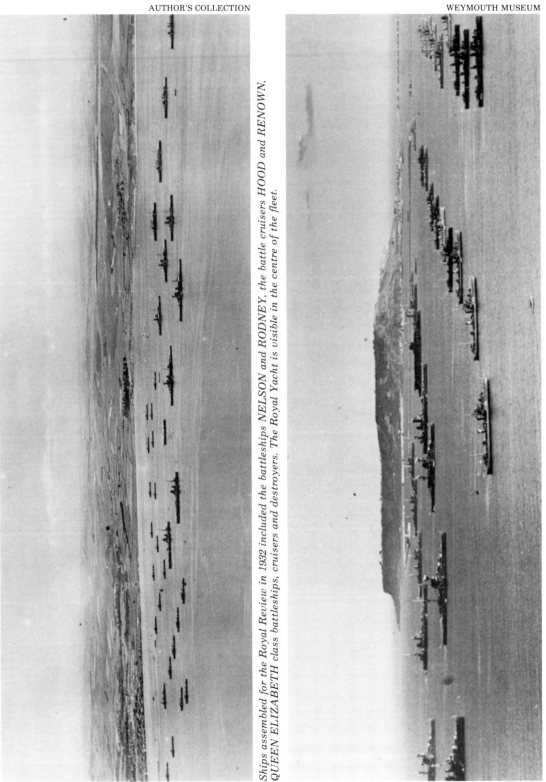

Ships assembled for the Royal Review in 1932 included the battleships NELSON and RODNEY, the battle cruisers HOOD and RENOWN, QUEEN ELIZABETH class battleships, cruisers and destroyers. The Royal Yacht is visible in the centre of the fleet.

The Home Fleet assembled in Weymouth Bay for review by His Majesty King George VI in 1938.

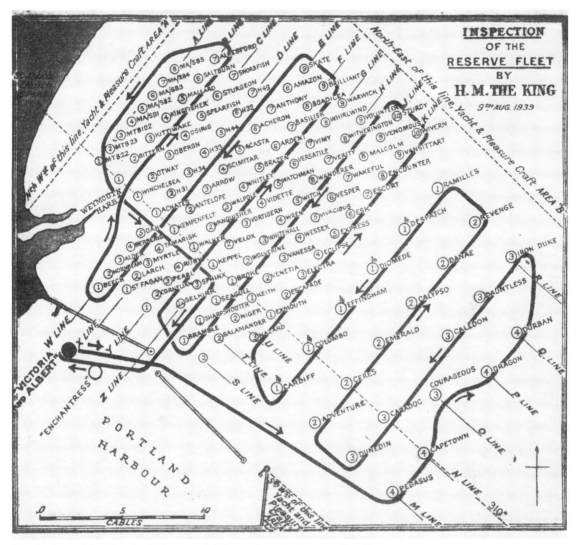

INSPECTION
OF THE
RESERVE FLEET
BY
H.M. THE KING
9TH AUG. 1939

The Review of the Fleet in 1939 . . . and this was just the Reserve Fleet!!

The Cruiser EFFINGHAM, Flagship of the C-in-C Reserve Fleet, Vice-Admiral Sir Max Horton, at the Royal review of his Fleet in Weymouth Bay, August 1939.

Home Fleet was Admiral Sir Charles Forbes, flying his flag in HMS *Nelson*. Her sister ship the *Rodney* was in the battle fleet together with the *Royal Oak*, *Royal Sovereign*, *Revenge* and *Ramillies*. The older cruiser HMS *Cornwall* and the newly commissioned cruisers *Southampton*, *Glasgow*, *Sheffield*, *Newcastle* and *Aurora* were present with destroyer flotillas. The lone aircraft carrier was HMS *Courageous*.

During exercises before the King, the ships fired at a radio controlled de Havilland 'Queen Bee' target aircraft, and mock attacks on the ships were carried out by 18 Fairey 'Swordfish' torpedo bombers.

Just as the assembly of a great fleet at Portland heralded the approach of war in 1914, so, twenty five years later, the Reserve Fleet gathered in Weymouth Bay. Once again war with Germany seemed certain.

On Wednesday 9 August 1939, King George VI came to Weymouth once more to review His Majesty's ships. He had travelled from Balmoral and embarked at Bincleaves Pier to join the Royal Yacht *Victoria and Albert*. Later that morning, when he left to visit the aircraft carrier *Courageous*, he was accompanied by the First Lord of the Admiralty, Lord Stanhope; Admiral Sir Dudley Pound, First Sea Lord; Captain Lord Louis Mountbatten, ADC to the King; and Admiral Darlan, Chief of the French Naval Staff. Aboard the *Courageous*, the Royal party was welcomed by Vice Admiral Sir Max Horton, in command of the Reserve Fleet. During the morning the King also visited the cruisers *Effingham* and *Cardiff* and the destroyer *Exmouth*. In the afternoon he embarked again in the Royal Barge for passage round the fleet which stretched in lines across Weymouth Bay.

More than 130 ships were assembled for

The paddle steamer MONARCH goes astern out of Weymouth harbour carrying libertymen back to their ships. When the fleet was in, the Cosens paddlers were kept busy ferrying ships' companies to and fro.

this review, of which no fewer than 42 would be sunk in the impending conflict. The *Courageous* had but a few weeks to live. Some ships, like the *Ardent, Acasta, Glowworm, Achates* and *Bramble* would be lost in action against German surface ships. The destroyers *Electra* and *Encounter* would be destroyed by the Japanese in the Java Sea. Many of the ships would be lost in the long hard campaign against the U-boats. By the end of 1940, four of the submarines present would be lost on operations. The flagship *Effingham* was destined to sink after striking an uncharted rock off Norway. The tragic list of ships lost showed the worldwide range of the Royal Navy's commitment, from home waters to the Barents Sea in the north, and southwards through the Mediterranean to far eastern seas, as well as the North and South Atlantic.

By the evening of that day, the King had left and the ships' companies, following the strenuous activities of the previous week, prepared to sail the ships to their war stations.

While the fleet was in, sailors in their hundreds were given leave ashore. Some strolled outside the dockyard gates at Portland, where, in a hundred yards frontage, the Albert Inn, the Royal Breakwater Hotel, the Sailors' Return , the Portland Roads' Hotel and the Jolly Sailor, waited to receive them. Others were brought to Weymouth in liberty boats that included Cosens paddle steamers. Some Weymouth pubs were out of bounds, but the men found plenty of alternatives. It was not unknown for the pubs to have run out of beer by lunch time, whereupon the publican had to send to the brewers for more. Royal Sailors' Rests were established by the much loved Aggie Weston, both at Portland and Weymouth. The Portland establishment remains.

In addition to the visiting ships of the Home Fleet, there was a substantial number of smaller naval vessels at Portland by 1936. Apart from the Anti-submarine Flotilla, the 1st Minesweeping Flotilla was at the base as well as a flotilla of ten Gem class trawlers. Three years later the patrol and training flotillas had increased to include the Fishery Protection Flotilla, 1st and 6th Minesweeping Flotillas, the 6th Submarine Flotilla attached to the depot ship *Titania* and a reserve flotilla of three submarines with the depot ship *Alecto*.

AUTHOR'S COLLECTION

3 weeks after the Review the aircraft carrier COURAGEOUS was lost—on 17th September 1939.

6

THE SECOND WORLD WAR—THE DEFENSIVE

The guns of the East Wears battery could train and fire on suspicious vessels approaching the entrance to Portland Harbour from the south.

The imminent outbreak of war led to the appointment of Rear Admiral the Hon E R Drummond CB MVO as Flag Officer in Charge at Portland. He took up his post in August 1939. He was born in 1884, the third son of Viscount Strathallan. After training in HMS *Britannia* he joined the cruiser *Caroline* in 1914 and served in the cruiser *Cardiff* from 1917 to 1919. He was promoted Commander in 1918 and Captain in 1926. His appointments included Chief of Staff to the Commander in Chief Portsmouth, and service in the cruisers *Delhi, Despatch, Curacoa, Dunedin* and *Achilles*. He became Rear Admiral and ADC to the King in 1936. He served on the New Zealand Station from 1935 until he retired in 1938. He was Flag Officer in Charge, Portland, from 1939 until 1942, being made Vice Admiral in 1940. He died in 1965. He had one son and two daughters, his son being lost in 1944 when HM Submarine *Sickle* was sunk, probably mined off the Greek coast.

An early task for the Flag Officer in Charge was the establishment of an examination service and contraband control. The function of the examination service was to identify and ascertain the character and intentions of vessels seeking entrance to a British port, and to give warning of any attempted entry by unfriendly or suspicious ships. Warnings were issued to masters against the unauthorised use of wireless and they had to comply with local regulations. An examination anchorage was established in Weymouth Bay and Rear Admiral Drummond was responsible for the chartering and fitting out of examination vessels. Ships brought into service included the Cosens paddle steamers *Empress, Victoria, Monarch* and *Embassy*, together with the locally owned tug *Marina*. The Breakwater Fort six inch gun battery kept a gun trained on an incoming vessel until she hoisted the correct signal indicating that she could be identified as friendly. The six inch guns at the Nothe were available in sup-

The yacht ST MODWEN was hired by the Admiralty in September 1939 and armed. Here she lies close to steamers awaiting contraband control. December 1939.

port. Detailed procedures were laid down in a booklet issued in 1938 by Admiral of the Fleet the Earl of Cork and Orrery, Commander in Chief, Portsmouth, and General A P Wavell, General Officer, Southern Command.

Contraband control was established at Weymouth on 25 August 1939. Cargoes of merchant ships were examined for material likely to help Germany's war effort. The guardship *London* was assisted by six smaller vessels. One of the first merchantmen examined is said to have carried twenty bags of coffee addressed to Hitler! By the end of February 1940, 141,237 tons of cargo had been seized at Weymouth.

On 3 September, the day war was declared, the aircraft carrier *Hermes* was in Portland harbour with the oiler *Limol* alongside. At 1000 that Sunday morning, the 12th Destroyer Flotilla left harbour, and at 1027 the oiler was cast off from the carrier, whose log recorded at 1100 that "Great Britain commenced hostilities with Germany".

Just as Lord Louis Mountbatten was at Portland at the beginning of World War II so he had been there at the end of World War I

as First Lieutenant of the patrol vessel *P 31*.

The new destroyer *Kelly* had arrived from Portsmouth on 31 August, under the command of Captain Lord Louis Mountbatten, to work up to full efficiency. She had already engaged in torpedo trials, gun drills and night exercises, but at the hour war was declared, all hands were employed painting the ship's side dark grey. On 4 September, together with other ships from Portland, both the *Kelly* and the *Hermes* were at sea. The *Hermes*, with her paravanes spread against moored mines, practised zigzagging at high speed before commencing flying practice. The *Kelly*, twelve and a half miles off Portland Bill during the afternoon, fired a single depth charge over a submarine contact. This may have been Lieutenant Commander W R Fell's submarine *H 31*, which had itself left harbour on the outbreak of hostilities. The aircraft carrier *Courageous* had left Portland on 2 September, never to return. She was torpedoed and sunk to the west of Ireland on 17 September. On 4 September the battleship *Ramillies* arrived from Scapa to await instructions before escorting a troop convoy to the Mediterranean. Ships of the Channel

A German aircraft passing over Portland took this photograph in October 1939. The Germans identified the ships as 4a CALEDON class cruisers 4b CERES class cruisers while the destroyers were described as JAVELIN class.

Force, the battleships *Resolution* and *Revenge*, the cruisers *Ceres*, *Caradoc* and *Cairo*, together with destroyers and submarines were already based at Portland. The responsibility of this Force was to cover the transport of men and munitions to the French ports, and to guard the western approaches to the English Channel.

The functions of the Portland sub-Command were to be a base for the Channel Force, a naval anchorage, a naval storage depot, and a convoy assembly point as re-quired. The Channel Force did not remain after the end of September, but the examination and contraband control continued, as did anti-submarine training, officer training in anti-submarine trawlers and drifters, and the working up of newly commissioned ships. Allied naval personnel were included in courses at Osprey: for example a Polish officer and twenty ratings began instruction in March 1940 before going on to join the ships' companies of two MASB (Motor Anti-Submarine Boats) and the destroyer *Garland*.

IMPERIAL WAR MUSEUM

Portland was a very busy base. In addition to training programmes and working up, a boom defence was being installed to protect ships inside the harbour from torpedo attack. Trawlers began the regular task of minesweeping. Rear Admiral Drummond was unhappy with the resources available to him. He felt he was unable to maintain a proper defence scheme for the area with inner and outer patrols. At first he had only four unarmed trawlers and two of these were withdrawn in December 1939 to reinforce the minesweeping forces on the East Coast. The anti-aircraft defences of the base were regarded as 'painfully thin'. There was also the need to maintain constant vigilance against U-boat activity.

Admiral Sir W M James, Commander in Chief, Portsmouth, believed that the Germans were unlikely to operate submarines in the English Channel, where there would be plenty of small craft and aircraft to hunt and observe submarines. At the same time the whole of the Atlantic was open to them, with merchantmen of necessity passing through focal points. He even went so far as to guess that no enemy submarine would be seen in the Channel unless it was damaged and trying to return to Germany by the shortest route. His assessment was not immediately justified.

At a conference between Hitler and the German Naval Staff on 23 September 1939, it was reported that mines had been laid by a

A newly completed corvette, possibly HMS GARDENIA or ARABIS, during work up off Portland in the early months of the war.

At the outbreak of war the seaward defences were the responsibility of the Dorset Heavy Regiment, Royal Artillery. There were two 9.2 inch guns at Blacknor, two 6 inch guns at the breakwater fort and two more at the Nothe fort. Four 12 pdr guns were sited on the Nothe, two at the Verne, one close to the Whitehead torpedo works, one at Ringstead and one at HMS *Osprey*. Two 2 pdr pompoms were placed near the oil fuel depot, two at HMS *Osprey*, one at Portland cemetery and one at Castletown Pier. Until the end of September, the ships of the Channel Force supplemented the anti-aircraft defences of the harbour.

U-boat in the approaches of some of the many possible British ports of departure, such as Weymouth and Dover. However, they could not be sure which were being used for the departure of British troops and their equipment. In fact the first convoys sailed in early September from Southampton to Cherbourg and from the Bristol Channel to Nantes and Saint Nazaire. The whole operation was carried out without loss. The mines had their effect, however, in bringing the first realities of war to Portland. The U-boat *U 26*, commanded by Kapitain Leutnant Klaus Ewerth, laid her mines in the general area of the Shambles, and on the night of 15 September the Belgian ship *Alex Van Opstal* (5900 tons) became her first victim. Returning from New York to Antwerp the Belgian vessel struck a mine five miles east of the Shambles lightship. The ship was plunged into darkness, broke in two just forward of the bridge and began to sink. The crew of 59 and eight passengers were safely taken off in her own lifeboats and put aboard the Greek ship *Atlanticos* before being put ashore at Weymouth. On 7 October the Dutch merchantman *Binnendijk* (6800 tons) was mined in the same area. She was also on passage from New York, this time to Rotterdam and had altered course towards Weymouth for examination. The ship caught fire but the crew were taken off safely before she went down bow first. The Greek ship *Elena R* (4500 tons) was sunk on 22 November two miles south of the Shambles lightship, and the fourth victim of U-boat mines was the patrol vessel *Kittiwake*, damaged on 20 September, again close to the Shambles.

A report to the Fuhrer on 10 October stated:

> Mine warfare off Weymouth and the Bristol Channel has achieved success; evidently the British have no minesweeping facilities.

Early in 1940 *U 48* laid a new minefield off Portland.

The German introduction of the magnetic mine required urgent counter measures. Portland dockyard workers were given orders to manufacture 'skids'. These were wooden rafts carrying heavy copper coils. If these rafts located a mine, they were usually destroyed in the explosion. However, in February 1940 the dockyard began manufacturing degaussing cables. These cables encircled the hulls of ships and an electric current was passed through them, reversing the ship's magnetic field and so preventing the activation of the magnetic mine. Such was the demand for magnetic coils that the governors of the Portland Borstal Institution were approached, with the result that all the boys were put at the disposal of the naval authorities and began the manufacture of the coils in large

sheds at the institution. For large vessels some 25-30 miles of cable might be required. Degaussing cables were fitted by Royal Navy personnel, some of whom occupied the buildings of Weymouth College under the name of HMS *Kredemnon*, the Greek for 'Magic Circle'. Eight ships were 'coiled' in March 1940 and the number rose to thirty one in April. Three German magnetic mines were exploded off Portland at the end of June.

The period from September 1939 until 10 May 1940 was designated by Winston Churchill as 'The Twilight War'. It came to a dramatic end with the invasion of Holland and Belgium. But even during those early months, while the land war was relatively quiet, there was plenty of naval activity in the English Channel, with a number of submarine sightings, real or imagined, some losses, but no interference from the air. The perspective of the war changed for Portland sub command following the blitzkrieg that brought the German army to the Channel coast in the spring and early summer of 1940. The Dutch army surrendered on 13 May and Paris fell on 14 June. On 22 June the French surrendered. The evacuation from Dunkirk, Operation Dynamo, began on 18 May and was completed by 4 June. Ships from Portland were called to help lift the Allied troops from the beaches. Afterwards *MASB 6, 7* and *10*, and the trawlers *Kindred Star, Thrifty, Topaze, Olvina* and *Elna* returned to the base. Operation Aerial, the evacuation of British and Allied troops from north west France began on 15 June. Evacuation took place from the French ports of Cherbourg, St Malo, Brest, St Nazaire and La Pallice. Of these, Cherbourg and St Malo were the responsibility of the Commander in Chief Portsmouth, Admiral Sir William James. He decided that he had insufficient escort vessels to provide proper protection for the troopships and they were therefore sailed independently. Troopships sailed for Southampton, coasters for Poole and smaller vessels for Weymouth. The remaining three evacuation ports came under the command of the Commander in Chief, Western Approaches, Admiral Sir Martin Dunbar-Nasmith, V.C. whose headquarters were at Plymouth.

Already the harbours at Portland and Weymouth had experience of handling refugees. Between 8 May and 3 June, the GWR Chief Docks Manager at Weymouth reported the arrival at Weymouth of 3784 refugees and 'hundreds of bicycles'. They were landed from the passenger ships *Canterbury, Maid of Orleans, Brittany* and *Volendam*, as well as from about 70 Belgian drifters, mainly from Zeebrugge and Ostend. Special trains took the refugees from Weymouth Quay to Paddington. Between 31 May and 20 June, the Chief Docks Manager reported the arrival of 15,814 British and Allied troops in thirty vessels, and the embarkation of 9,156 French troops to return to their homeland. Finally, in the period from 20 to 28 June, 25,484 evacuees came ashore from the Channel Islands. Twenty ships came from Jersey, thirty from Guernsey and five from Alderney.

In early June the German air force made its presence felt by minelaying operations on five nights between 2 and 13 June, and as the month passed the French airfields close to the Channel coast received squadrons of fighters and bombers. On 9 June as the newly converted auxiliary anti-aircraft ship *Foylebank* arrived at Portland, a mine was exploded by the trawler sweeping a clear passage for her into the harbour. In the early hours of 20 June bombs fell close to Whitehead Pier, Ferry Bridge, Osmington and in West Bay. This raid was more of a reconnaisance than a serious attack. The estimated six aircraft seemed to make a landfall at Portland Bill, circle Weymouth Bay, then head northwards towards inland objectives. On the evening of the last day of June, three German bombers dropped their bombs on the Verne and Chesil, and so, with the month of July, a new chapter of warfare began for Portland, not only involving the Luftwaffe but also E boats—fast motor torpedo boats—newly arrived at their bases on the French Channel Coast. As a

salient jutting out into the Channel, Portland was only 15-20 minutes flying time from the airfields in Normandy. The naval base was itself under threat from these forces, as were the Channel convoys and the movement of warships. Finally, and most serious of all, there was the threat of a German invasion.

In the first days of July the work of the naval base continued without interruption. In the harbour the ships included two Dutch submarines *O 9* and *O 10*, carrying out anti-submarine training, the armed yacht *Brinmatic*, and a number of merchant ships. The corvette *Geranium* had completed her work up on 24 June and her sister ship *Mallow* left on 2 July. The 5500 ton *Foylebank* remained.

HMS *Foylebank* (Capt. H P Wilson RN) was built in 1930. A merchantman of the Bank Line, she was converted after the outbreak of war by Harland and Wolff at Belfast to become an anti-aircraft ship. She mounted eight 4 inch AA guns in twin shields, two four barrelled pompoms and several machine guns. On arrival at Portland she regularly lay at 'A' buoy.

The morning of 4 July began pleasantly enough. A moderate wind blew from the north west and visibility was good with some blue sky clouding a little. The *Foylebank's* ship's company were carrying out normal routine and half the ship's armament was manned. The first hint of trouble came at 0825, when the ship's own warning system, codenamed 'Cuckoo', reported aircraft bearing 150 degrees thirty or forty miles away. Three minutes later RAF Fighter Command headquarters at Uxbridge reported a plot of six plus aircraft. The *Foylebank* came to immediate readiness and at 0835 reported that the machines were only fifteen miles distant. This was followed by reports that RAF fighters were coming down from the north. At 0840 the German formation appeared, some twenty Junkers 87 in two columns, line astern at 5000 feet. Though correctly identified by the starboard bridge look-out, an officer at first thought that the aircraft were Lysanders of the RAF. Close to the harbour

FOYLEBANK ASSOCIATION

HMS FOYLEBANK, *badly damaged and with heavy casualties, burns and settles onto the bottom of Portland Harbour on the morning of 4 July 1940. Converted to become an auxilliary anti-aircraft ship, she was working up at Portland when attacked. Soon after the sinking her armament was removed. Later she was lifted in two sections and towed away for scrap.*

*The last moments . . .
the funeral pyre
of the FOYLEBANK.*

FOYLEBANK ASSOCIATION

68

the Stukas broke formation and dived on their targets, most of them heading for the *Foylebank*, immobile at her mooring. Down they came in quick succession, firing their machine guns, and releasing their bombs at the bottom of the dive. The attack was ferocious and short. It lasted only eight minutes and in that time the *Foylebank* was hit repeatedly. The ship opened fire. A and B turrets had hardly begun firing when they were put out of action as bombs fell between the ship's bridge and guns. B turret was lifted off its platform by the blast. Y turret managed to get off more than twenty rounds from each barrel. Shells were fused for 'close barrage' and two of them burst directly beneath the second bomber to attack. In the explosions, ammunition came adrift from the ready use lockers. The shells were grabbed as they came to hand.

The pompoms and machine guns fired until the ship was abandoned. At the starboard pompom Leading Seaman Jack Mantle continued to fire his gun by hand firing gear after the electrical power failed. His left leg was shattered by a bomb explosion and he suffered multiple injuries. The rest of the gun's crew were killed or wounded, but Mantle continued firing until the end of the action when he collapsed by his gun, only two barrels of which were working. Mortally wounded, he was placed by his comrades on some coconut matting and passed aboard a tug that had come alongside. There, on the deck of the tug, he died. Jack Mantle was awarded a posthumous Victoria Cross for his heroism, the first ever to be awarded in British home waters. Leading Seaman Cousins and Leading Seaman Gould, who were also serving the ship's close range weapons, received the Distinguished Service Medal. As the attacking bombers climbed away from the stricken *Foylebank*, fires started by their accurate bombing soon began to take hold amidships. Rescue vessels came alongside and took off the wounded and other survivors, but by 1000 that morning the ship was settling by the stern and exploding ammunition forced the rescuers away. As the morning passed, the ship sank lower and lower and a thick pall of smoke rose and drifted westwards across the bay, visible for miles. The *Foylebank* became a total loss. Of her ship's company of 300, 13 officers and 144 men were saved.

The merchant ship *City of Melbourne* was also at anchor in Portland harbour and the *Foylebank* was the nearest ship to her. The first her captain knew of the attack was the sound of machine gun fire, quickly followed by seven bombs falling within eight feet of the ship in a line on the port side. Everything aboard shook violently. The wireless was put out of action, all wash basins and glass were broken, the compasses dislodged and the engine room flooded. The force of the explosions cleared all the plates of rust. The ship had to be towed into shallow water.

The steamship *East Wales* (4300 tons),

The mortal remains of Leading Seaman Jack Mantle rest in the naval cemetery overlooking the harbour where he won his Victoria Cross.

AUTHOR'S COLLECTION

bound from Freetown to London with a cargo of maize was lying in the harbour a mile from the shore. Two bombs fell eight feet from the stern of the ship while another large bomb dropped ten feet off the port side opposite the engine room, causing considerable damage. The planes that attacked her flattened out from their dive and flew away over land.

At no time during the raid did RAF fighters appear. Indeed the speed and accuracy of the attack demonstrated that unless fighter protection over the base could be assured, then operations from Portland would have to be curtailed and possibly discontinued altogether. The nearest operational fighter station that day was at Middle Wallop on Salisbury Plain. Much closer to Portland was the airfield and gunnery training school at Warmwell. This grass airfield was, on the very day that the *Foylebank* was sunk, declared ready for operational use. Fighters based there would in the future have a better chance of intercepting raids directed at Portland provided they had sufficient warning to enable them to gain height. Unfortunately, the coastal radar chain did not extend far enough westwards to ensure such early warning. The radar station at Ventnor could detect some approaching raids and there was a nearer station at Worth Matravers. Early in July, 609 Spitfire Squadron was posted to Middle Wallop, where 238 Hurricane Squadron was already working up. On 12 July, 152 Spitfire Squadron flew south from Acklington to Warmwell itself. These squadrons, supported by others from as far west as Exeter, fought valiantly in defence of Portland and the coastal convoys throughout the Battle of Britain.

A short memorial service was held alongside the wrecked *Foylebank* on the afternoon of Sunday 7 July. The attack had demonstrated that an anti-aircraft vessel could not be used as part of the anti-aircraft defences of a weakly protected harbour. The Flag Officer-in-Charge, Portland, reported to the Admiralty that the *Foylebank's* anti-aircraft guns did not seem to have suffered much and

that salvage should be easy. The forepart of the ship was salvaged in December 1943 and towed alongside the southern breakwater. The remains of the wreck were not removed until 1952, when a recovery party began work under the command of Captain W R Fell RN who had been a Commander in charge of HM Submarine *H 31* at Portland in September 1939. Based on the salvage vessel *Kinbrace*, they began to clear the remains of the wreck. The *Foylebank's* holds were loaded with stone ballast and fifty gallon oil drums. The drums were supposed to give the ship additional buoyancy but they had collapsed under water pressure as the ship lay on the harbour bottom. Rotting stores, ammunition and unexploded German bombs were found on board and the remains of some of the ship's company were discovered in the living quarters.

After removing the oil drums, divers patched holes made by the bombs that struck the ship in 1940 and cut away the decks to reach the main engines. Finally the stone ballast was removed. At last the remains of the ship were floated and the *Foylebank*, under tow, made her last voyage to a ship breaker's yard on the river Thames.

Air raids continued. On the same afternoon that the service took place alongside the Foylebank, the minesweeper HMS *Jeannie Deans* reported that she was being attacked by aircraft south of St Albans Head, then that three German bombers were approaching Portland. These machines, Heinkel 111s, crossed Chesil Beach near the oil tanks and turned to the south east. Damage was small from bombs that were dropped but another paddler minesweeper, HMS *Mercury*, was hit abreast her foremost gun. There were nine casualties aboard the ship. Men were also injured aboard the tanker *British Inventor* which was narrowly missed by a bomb, some twenty of which fell into the water within the harbour.

Early the next morning a single Heinkel 111 came from the landward side and dropped its bombs into the harbour. Although this machine was identified by the Observer Corps as hostile, Royal Air Force plotters marked it as doubtful. Indeed it was still being plotted as doubtful when it dropped its bombs.

The submarine tender HMS *Warrior II*, once a famous luxury yacht, was bombed and sunk on the morning of 11 July while some twelve miles east of Portland Bill. At noon the same day raiders attacked Portland, dropping bombs close to the floating dock and slightly damaging two small vessels. The following day six bombs were dropped by a lone aircraft close to the coaling jetty, causing some settlement.

The vulnerability of the Shambles lightship had to be considered. The light itself would be an aid to navigation for German bombers and E boats. From 1 August the light was extinguished and the crew and stores from the ship were landed at Weymouth. The lightship herself was towed into Portland five days later.

The vulnerability of warships to air attack was further demonstrated during July. Not only was the converted merchant ship *Foylebank* sunk at her moorings, but fast, independent destroyers, with sea room in which to manoeuvre, were overcome.

The destroyer *Beagle* (Lt Cdr R H Wright) was on passage from Dover to Devonport on 20 July when she was attacked by two squadrons, each of ten Junkers Ju 87 dive bombers 10 miles off Portland Bill. The enemy aircraft crossed astern of the ship at about 8000 feet. While the first squadron flew on northwards, the second turned as soon as it was astern and dived to the attack. On sighting the enemy, the *Beagle* quickly built up to full speed, zig-zagging and keeping the wind before the beam. The bombers, led with great skill and determination by the squadron leader, pressed home the attack, but no bombs hit the ship. Some fell 250 yards away but others were as close as 30 feet. Bomb splinters spattered aboard as some bombs exploded on contact with the sea, while others burst some ten feet below the surface. The ship was fortunate to escape with slight damage to the port steering unit, while a seam was opened in the foremost boiler room and the electric leads to B gun were cut.

The destroyer's ability to combat the dive bombers was limited. The bombers flew above the maximum elevation of the 4.7 inch guns, though the pompoms were in continuous action. It was reckoned that a 3 inch high angle gun could have been used with great effect. The *Beagle* survived.

HMS *Delight* did have a 3 inch high angle gun when she sailed from Portsmouth for the Clyde on 29 July. Her progress down channel was observed by the newly installed Freya radar situated near Auderville on the Hague peninsula. At 1835 when the destroyer was some twenty miles south of Portland Bill she was attacked by a formation of Junkers Ju 87 dive bombers. The 3 inch anti-aircraft gun

The destroyer DELIGHT received no direct hits, but was sunk by near misses when dive bombed on 29 July, 1940.

and the multiple machine guns on the wings of the bridge opened fire. Captain M Fogg Elliott, who had commanded the ship throughout the Norwegian campaign, had already earned the respect of the ship's company by the manner in which he had manoeuvred the ship under heavy air attack. Once more he turned and twisted the *Delight* with sufficient skill to avoid any direct hits on the ship, but the near misses did mortal damage. Bombs exploding below the surface of the sea fractured the forward fuel tank which caught fire.

The destroyers *Vansittart* and *Broke* were despatched at once from Devonport, but the four available high speed coastal craft from Portland were easily first to the scene. *ML 102, ML 105, MASB 1* and *MASB 5* were in Portland or Weymouth harbours when, at about 1930, they received signals to proceed to the aid of the stricken destroyer. Leaving some members of their crews ashore, the craft left their berths within five minutes and headed towards the *Delight* at speeds up to 27 knots. They could see smoke rising on the horizon. At 2025, *ML 105* and *MASB 5* reached the destroyer and found her burning furiously. Ammunition was exploding forward, and a sudden big explosion from B gun magazine blew the gun high into the air.

Captain Fogg Elliott ordered the wounded to be taken aboard *ML 105* and the little craft cast off with about 70 survivors, reaching Portland at 2230. Five minutes later *MASB 5* came in with 50 survivors, while *MASB 1* found a man floating some three hundred yards from the destroyer.

Meanwhile *ML 102* lay with her bows against the *Delight*, and Captain Fogg Elliott enquired if the sinking destroyer could more quickly be sent to the bottom by depth charge. The launch took off the remaining seven officers and eight crew, circled a while and then dropped a depth charge four feet astern of the destroyer. The explosion blew her fittings flat but did not seem to damage the hull. *MASB 1*, however, reported that at 2210 only the bows of the ship could be seen

above the surface at ninety degrees.

Their Lordships at the Admiralty were displeased at the loss of another destroyer so soon after the heavy casualties in this class of ship during the evacuation from Dunkirk. Immediately after receiving reports of the attack, a signal was sent to CinC Portsmouth asking why the *Delight* had sailed at 1426 that day instead of at dusk. Admiral Sir William James replied that he had no hesitation in sailing single destroyers with full manoeuvrability if the situation required it. But it remained the opinion of A V Alexander, First Lord, and Admiral Sir Dudley Pound, First Sea Lord that an error of judgement was committed in sailing her by day.

A particularly fierce raid on Portland occurred on Sunday 11 August. The day was fine with bright sunshine and high cloud. At 0945 Ventnor radar reported a heavy build up

The Battle of Britian is at its height as bombs fall across the Chequered Fort towards dockyard installations at Portland.

of Luftwaffe machines over Cherbourg. This formation consisted of more than 150 aircraft, including at least 50 Junkers 88s, 20 Heinkel 111s, 60 Messerschmitt Bf 110s and 30 Messerschmitt Bf 109s which began to approach Portland from the south and south east. The fighters flew ahead and high above the bombers, presumably to draw the defending Spitfires and Hurricanes away from the bombers and involve them in dog fights. The plan succeeded since most of the attacking RAF machines went for the circle of Messerschmitts, while only a few attacked the bombers. Six squadrons of fighter aircraft became involved in the battle. The Heinkels dropped their bombs from 15,000 feet but the Junkers 88 dive bombers dived on the naval installations from 10,000 feet converging from different directions in groups of three to six aircraft. At 1028 the first bombs fell, thirty two landing on Portland Admiralty property, three on the Royal Naval Torpedo Depot at Weymouth, while a number fell into the sea off Bincleaves, HMS *Osprey* and in Balaclava Bay.

Two oil tanks were pierced, one of them catching fire. A bomb falling near no 3 tank set fire to a wooden building and the flames ignited oil flowing from the punctured tank. The grass enclosure began to burn and the smoke and flames made the road impassable. Portland Fire Brigade soon had the blaze under control and oil could then be pumped from the damaged tank into the empty one standing next to it. The main oil pipe line was fractured in three places and it was estimated that 150-200 tons of oil were lost. Damage was caused to the railway line between Portland and Weymouth, the Junior Surgeon's quarters at the Royal Naval Hospital were hit and the Captain, Anti-Submarine's office was set on fire. At Bincleaves the shipwright's shop was wrecked. In the harbour the destroyer *Scimitar* and *ML 102* were slightly damaged by several near misses. The floating dock was holed and strained, though the trawler HMS *Hertfordshire*, in the dock at the time, was refloated without damage. In

the same raid, 58 bombs fell on the borough of Weymouth.

In the air battle there were heavy losses on both sides, especially in the dogfight between the fighters. Five of the Junkers 88s were destroyed, one of them crashing on Portland almost intact. As a postscript, one of the Hurricane fighters shot down that day was not recovered from the Fleet behind Chesil Beach until 1983.

On 13 August large numbers of aircraft flew overhead above the clouds. Although there were fierce air battles no bombs fell on Portland. But the following day the Verne Citadel was hit and other bombs fell in and around the dockyard. Some damage was done to the coaling pier, the tug *Carbon* and the patrol vessel *Kingfisher*. Just outside the dockyard itself considerable damage was done to Admiralty House and No 2 Residence. No naval casualties were reported but there were civilian casualties when bombs fell on the Borstal buildings and the wireless transmitting station. The next afternoon three Junkers 88s carried out a low level bombing attack, causing damage to the coaling jetty, the railway line and the recreation ground. There were no casualties. Anti aircraft guns opened fire, but ceased as the three bombers climbed rapidly into the clouds. The unfortunate impression was given that the guns ceased firing because bombs were falling. The speed of the German attack meant that the bombs exploded as the bombers disappeared.

During the air battles fought over Weymouth Bay and out into the Channel off Portland, many aircraft crashed into the sea and their pilots and crews baled out. Arrangements were made for all available MASB and ML to proceed to sea on the receipt of air raid warning red and to wait for orders as to possible rescue.

Though there was almost daily air activity throughout August, it was not until mid September that the naval base received its next damaging attack. The bombers came on the afternoon of 15 September, when some 25

Heinkel He 111s approached from the south east at 16,000 feet and attacked the base down sun. The bombers had no fighter escort. High explosive and incendiary bombs were dropped. The Admiralty incline railway was damaged, a water main fractured, a boom defence shed was damaged and the wall of the breakwater was severely cracked. Windows, doors and roofs of the Anti-Submarine establishment as well as test buildings also received damage. Unfortunately four 3.7″ anti aircraft guns at Southwell had been removed on 11 September, as had the four guns at Wyke. To make matters worse, only six fighters were sent up as the number of hostile bombers was estimated at six. Even so, Spitfires of 152 Squadron from Warmwell shot down one Heinkel of KG55 and damaged another.

Enemy air attacks continued during 1941. During January and February German night bombers passed over the base to raid British towns and cities, including Bristol and Swansea. On the night of January 16 a single plane dropped four high explosive bombs near HMS *Attack* at the old Osprey buildings; later another dropped four bombs into the sea near the breakwater. A low level raid in cloud and rain on 1 April damaged a number of aircraft at Warmwell airfield and caused casualties, and during the same month a number of light attacks were made on Portland. The diversion of major German air forces to the impending attack on Soviet Russia and to meet the demands of the Mediterranean theatre meant the withdrawal of many aircraft from France. The heavy raids of the past could not easily be mounted again, and throughout the rest of 1941 attacks on the naval base were made more often than not by single aircraft. In June a Junkers Ju 88, bombing from 500 feet, sank the coal hulk *Himalaya* in Portland harbour, while on the night of 15 July a single aircraft flew low along the northern arm of the breakwater and dropped bombs on the torpedo depot. They did not explode, but other bombs fell on the town of Weymouth. Another coal hulk was

sent to the bottom by a single aircraft when the *Hindustan* was hit. Once again it was a lone aircraft that hit the Whitehead Torpedo factory on 1 May when it dropped one 250 lb and 4 smaller bombs.

It was in the midst of the German air offensive that the German navy made its presence felt in a controversial episode involving the French liner *Meknes* (6,100 tons). When this ship left Southampton in the late afternoon of 24 July 1940, in addition to her crew of 104, she carried 1,180 passengers, most of whom were French servicemen being repatriated to their own country. They were men who wished to return to France rather than join the Free French forces in England. They were no longer combatants and the ship herself was unarmed, having had all guns and ammunition removed before the cross channel voyage began. As darkness fell, all the ship's lights were switched on. In addition to normal navigation and bridge lights, powerful projectors shone on French flags painted on the ship's sides while other lights shone on the French ensign flying aft. At 2255 machine gun fire was heard and tracer bullets were seen coming from the port side, a number of rounds hitting the liner. Captain D Dubroc stopped the ship, giving two long blasts on the ship's whistle and at the same time signalling her identity by Morse lamp. Ten minutes later, a torpedo fired by the German E boat *S 27*, commanded by Leutnant Klug, hit the *Meknes* on the port side between nos three and four holds, and all the ship's lights went out.

As the moon rose, orders were given to launch lifeboats and rafts. One lifeboat was riddled with bullets and sank immediately, while two others were probably overturned in launching. The ship at first settled by the stern, then broke in two and sank, all within eight minutes of being hit. Large quantities of wreckage came to the surface and many survivors clung to this. Fortunately the sea was calm with a clear sky and light wind.

A trawler and two MASB were sent from Portland to aid the rescue and RAF fighter protection was ordered at daybreak. The destroyers *Sabre* and *Shikari* from Portsmouth together with the *Wolverine* and *Viscount* from Western Approaches Command soon arrived on the scene of the sinking. By 0810 that morning they had picked up all the survivors in sight. They then set course for Weymouth where they transferred them to the boats already waiting to receive them. Altogether the destroyers brought in 99 officers, 796 men, 2 women and one child. Fifteen others were either picked up dead or had died before reaching Weymouth.

Those picked up by the *Wolverine* did not impress the ship's company:

> . . . of some 1100 souls rescued at sea by *Wolverine*, none before have been such an undisciplined, base and hysterical type. When the ship proceeded alongside the rafts and wreckage, those so able immediately swarmed aboard, leaving those incapacitated to be brought on board by the British sailors; very few appeared interested in anything else but their personal welfare.
>
> Though taken to the messdecks to be dried, clothed and given hot drinks, they raided the galley and took any further clothing they could lay their hands on, including blankets from the hammocks. They relieved themselves anywhere and quarrelled among themselves. Sentries were posted and pistols issued to the ship's officers and petty officers.
>
> After departure it was necessary to disinfect all compartments where survivors had been and remove buckets full of crockery, excrement and other filthy refuse.

All the survivors were disembarked in 35 minutes and then the destroyers sailed.

In contrast to the report from the *Wolverine*, Captain Dubroc of the *Meknes*, in his report, paid tribute to the calmness with which his crew behaved in the face of 'this cowardly attack'. The ship was hit just as all aboard thought they were quite safe, and it was Captain Dubroc's opinion that it was due to the fact that there were so many sailors among those being repatriated that such a large number of people were saved.

It was clearly expected that the *Meknes* would be guaranteed a safe passage back to France. Brilliantly lit, unarmed and unescorted the ship drew attention to herself and her peaceful progress. It must be presumed that the German naval authorities were informed of the sailing. If so, why was she attacked and sunk? It may be that the E boats concerned in the attack had not been told that the *Meknes* would be crossing the Channel that night, and even viewed her as a trap, in the Q ship tradition, designed to draw the E boats close to her before opening fire with hidden weapons. Whatever the cause, the loss in lives was considerable, Captain Dubroc estimating that 33 of his crew and about 300 of his passengers were missing.

The Threat of Invasion

In July and August 1940 the German High Command prepared a plan for the invasion of Britain. The initial assault would fall upon the coasts of Kent and Sussex, but included in the plan for Operation Sealion was a possible follow-up by the 6th Army from Cherbourg. This force would land in Lyme Bay and then capture Weymouth before advancing towards Bristol.

On the British side, it was expected that the German assault would be by the shortest route across the Channel. Naval forces would have to provide cover from the Wash to Newhaven and striking forces would be based at Humber, Harwich, Sheerness and Portsmouth or Dover. Vice-Admiral Drummond at Portland was faced with the deployment of his very limited resources to prevent, or at least delay, landings at Portland or Weymouth. In Weymouth harbour the old cargo vessel *Kenfig Pool* was to be used as a blockship. In July she twice exercised swinging across the harbour entrance. Further rehearsals were carried out in August, but in September, when invasion seemed imminent, she was placed in position each night. Pontoons were also acquired and rigged with chains to prevent any landing parties from getting alongside the piers. At Portland all shore lights were permanently extinguished. Three torpedo tubes were placed at the en-

The blockship KENFIG POOL dominates the buildings of Hope Quay in Weymouth harbour. The ship was prepared as a blockship in the event of a German invasion. She eventually left for Southampton in 1943.

trances to the harbour with live torpedoes in place. They were ready for firing by early August. Spikes were also fitted to the defences at the harbour entrances. From 1 November two striking forces of ships were formed, one of trawlers and one of motor boats. Each day, a patrol force, normally of three ships, anchored at noon in Weymouth Bay and later sailed on local patrol at the best speed the force could maintain. Throughout the period there were two stages of alert. The first was 'Stand by to man defences' and the second, 'Emergency—man dockyard defences.'

The anti-invasion patrol, though never confronted by a German assault on the Dorset coast, nevertheless suffered losses. HM trawler *Loch Monteith* was on such patrol on 24 September when, at 0245, there was an explosion forward. The damage was contained entirely in the bows forward of the collision bulkhead, but six men were killed in their sleeping quarters. The cause of the explosion was not known, but was assumed to be a mine.

The Commanding Officer, Lieutenant J R Simpson RNR, signalled to Portland Bill that the *Loch Monteith* had been mined ten miles west of the Bill. The tug *Pilot* was ordered to proceed to the inshore channel and *ML 105* left Weymouth to assist. The damaged trawler was brought safely to Portland. Two pieces of metal found on board were sent to the Research and Experiments Department at Princes Risborough. There the analysts concluded that the pieces appeared to be normal bomb fragments. This being so, it is possible that the *Loch Monteith* was victim of a gliding attack from a German bomber.

Four nights later the trawler HMS *Recoil* disappeared. She formed part of an anti-invasion patrol line of five trawlers at sea on a dark night but with good visibility and a slight sea. The *Recoil* acknowledged a signal late on the evening of 27 September, but from 0400 the next morning failed to respond to calls from base. As radio communication frequently failed there was no immediate concern, and since two other trawlers had collided it was thought that the *Recoil* might be escorting a damaged ship to Dartmouth. It was not until 1030 on 28 September that the Commander-in-Chief, Portsmouth was informed that the *Recoil* was missing.

A Lysander aircraft took off from Warmwell airfield and searched for two hours between Start Point and St Albans Head, but found nothing.

HM trawler *Angle*, whose patrol line was next to that of the *Recoil*, reported that a loud explosion was heard about 2116. It was of sufficient force to cause men to come on deck. It seemed like an underwater explosion. When the *Angle* reached the end of her patrol line nearest the *Recoil* there was a strong smell of paraffin or Diesel oil. The missing trawler, once the German *Blankenburg*, was Diesel driven.

The *Recoil* would not have been far from the position where the trawler *Loch Monteith* had been damaged, and it seemed likely that the unfortunate ship had been mined and lost with all hands. With no floating wreckage in sight there was some anxiety that she might have been captured, but late in October the body of a Sub Lieutenant from the *Recoil* was recovered from the sea. He had died from drowning.

At the beginning of 1941 it was thought that the Germans were still making preparations for the invasion of Britain. Vice Admiral Drummond issued a memorandum on 25 January 1941 entitled 'Defence of Portland Dockyard Area', in which the probable methods of attack were considered to be by airborne troops and aerial bombardment in conjunction with landings by seaborne forces in large and small craft at suitable beaches on or near Portland. Available defence forces included: 305th Holding Battalion stationed at the Verne Fort, the Dockyard Home Guard, Naval Personnel from HMS *Boscawen* and *Attack* and HM ships in Portland harbour.

The 305th Holding Battalion would establish its headquarters on the hill above the naval centre. A and B Companies were to defend the dockyard area and one company would remain in reserve at the Verne to counter attack as required. The two companies of the dockyard Home Guard were to take up defence positions near the rifle range, the *Osprey* football ground, Balaclava pillboxes, roads near the naval centre and victualling office, the dockyard motor transport garage and signal tower redoubt,

and the heads of the loading jetty, floating dock pier, the western arm and pens. There were also defence positions on the foreshore north of the dockyard main gate and on the Coaling Arm. The Home Guard would reinforce or relieve 305th Battalion as circumstances demanded. The naval personnel of HMS *Boscawen* and HMS *Attack* would man defences at their respective establishments in close co-operation with the B Company 305th Holding Battalion.

If invasion occurred ships at anchor were to raise steam with all despatch, go to action stations and cover by gunfire all approaches to the dockyard and Chesil Beach from the harbour. Ships unable to raise steam would be required to warp ship to bring their main armament to bear on the harbour and prevent landings on the pens or coaling jetty.

Non-combatants were to go home, or, if unable to get to Weymouth, they were to disperse to houses, quarries and other temporary shelter on Portland. It was the responsibility of the Marine Police to marshal and direct non-combatants to their dispersal points. Should siege conditions prevail, arrangements were put in hand to ration water to two gallons per head per day. So the preparations were made, never to be put to the ultimate test.

Portland harbour itself was further protected by a controlled minefield laid in April 1941. There were six lines of mines, each consisting of 12 Mark III type.

Although the threat of invasion steadily declined in 1941, and became very unlikely after the German invasion of Russia, nevertheless raids could be mounted. Anti-invasion forces therefore remained at the disposal of Portland Sub-command. At the beginning of 1942 these extended to the 4th and 20th ML flotillas (12 boats), the 4th MGB Flotilla (8 boats), 14 anti-submarine and minesweeping trawlers and two anti-submarine yachts, HMS *Rion* and *Star of India*. Provision having been made to counter any invasion attempt, the forces at Portland steadily assumed a less defensive posture and

Convoy in the Channel: ships were subjected to heavy air attack in the early stages of the Battle of Britain in 1940. Throughout the war, channel convoys were threatened by German E Boats and aircraft. Casualties were sometimes heavy.

turned to the offensive, the maintenance of convoys through the English Channel and the build-up towards the day when Allied forces would themselves form the invasion force and land on the shores of France.

The Channel Convoys

With the outbreak of hostilities the Admiralty took control of all movements of merchant shipping around the British Isles. A convoy system was introduced for the protection of trade against submarines. Ocean convoys, designated OA, sailed from Southend on alternate days, passing westwards down the English Channel. SL convoys, from Freetown in Sierra Leone, began on 14 September 1939. Later in the war, when

circumstances changed, CE and CW convoys began working each way along the channel coast serving the ports between Southend and the Bristol Channel. From July 1941 WP and PW convoys operated between the Bristol Channel and Portsmouth. These coastal convoys were not threatened by U-boats, but were often attacked by aircraft or E boats—or both. The Dover barrage, a minefield laid to prevent German warships and submarines from entering the Channel from the east was largely successful in ensuring the safe passage of convoys until the German occupation of the Low Countries and France in the early summer of 1940.

From the outbreak of war until the end of April 1940, 137 convoys sailed in the English Channel or the southern North Sea with a total of 1,777 ships, only one of which was lost by enemy action.

During the summer of 1940 sea traffic in the Channel received the fierce attentions of the Luftwaffe, often combined with attacks from the German coastal forces craft, the E boats. One which suffered particularly severely was the ocean convoy OA 178.

Convoy OA 178 left the Thames Estuary at 0745 on 3 July 1940. By noon next day the ships had taken up their ocean formation and had passed south of the Isle of Wight towards Portland, escorted by the corvette *Clarkia*. The zigzag course took some of the ships within sight of the French coast, estimated by the captain of the tanker *British Corporal* to be only fifteen miles away.

At 1255 the convoy was attacked by German bombers followed by a second attack at 1425. At 1516, after the attack was over, the convoy was ordered to proceed to Portland. The convoy Commodore informed the escort that some ships had been damaged and that his own ship *Peterton* was short of ammunition. The *Clarkia* herself reported that seven ships had been lost or seriously damaged. The convoy sailed into Weymouth Bay and the *Peterton* anchored at 2025, only to receive orders passed on by the escort that the convoy was to proceed to sea. Fifteen minutes later the convoy was under way again and heading out once more into the channel round Portland Bill.

The E boats attacked the vulnerable merchantmen at midnight. In quick succession the *Elmcrest, Britsum, British Corporal* and *Hartlepool* were torpedoed. Most of the crew of the *Hartlepool* also took to the boats. Captain Rogerson reported:

> At 0400 on the 5th, the three Belgian patrol boats steamed up to me from Portland and I hailed one to take off my injured men; he took them to Weymouth. I hailed the other two patrol boats and told them I was awaiting tugs. At 0700, a destroyer *H 21 (Scimitar)* came alongside and asked if he could take off my crew. I replied 'No; I am waiting for tugs'. Her captain informed me that the destroyer *H 18 (Sabre)* had 17 of my crew aboard including the Chief Officer. At 0740 a patrol boat, which I think was *No 154*, came alongside and hailed me. I told him I was awaiting tugs, but he advised me to abandon ship.

The risks in sailing westbound convoys through the English Channel were too great and they were discontinued. The Admiralty even determined that no ship should use the English Channel for trading directly between east and west coast ports. Permits would be issued where it was essential to maintain supplies, but in any case ships must not exceed 1600 tons gross. Such convoys of small ships might call at south coast ports, but convoy speeds had to be at least eight knots in fair weather.

South coast convoys were initiated in August solely to supply coal to ports on the south coast, and this was strictly adhered to until May 1941. Cycles of convoys sailed with a Channel Guard of teams of light machine gunners aboard ships in the convoy. Eight vessels were prepared to provide a mobile kite balloon barrage, the kites flying at 2,000 to 2,500 feet. These new coastal convoys, designated CE or CW, at first took an average of 25 days on their round trip, with delays being caused to individual ships by waiting for convoys, slow discharging and crew troubles. Later in the war, the round trip was reduced to 12 days but this excluded loading time.

The early CW convoys did not go unscathed. Convoy CW 9 was very seriously mauled.

The end of the Battle of Britain, and the onset of autumn and winter saw a dramatic reduction in the ferocity of the attacks on convoys in the English Channel. In the winter and throughout 1941 the coastal convoys, particularly important in delivering coal to the south coast ports, sailed regularly. At first they sailed every ten days but from May this was improved to an eight day cycle. Sometimes a convoy would stop in Weymouth Bay if the weather was particularly severe.

By the new year 1942, the CE and CW convoys sailed regularly with escorts of trawlers, supported between Falmouth and Portland by a destroyer of the Hunt class. The threat of attack increased with the improved weather of the summer months and with the deployment of Junkers 88 and Messerschmitt Me 110 aircraft against the ships. Convoy WP 183 suffered particularly heavily. The E boats of the 2nd Flotilla struck first. Seven boats, *S 48, S 50, S 63, S 67, S 70, S 104* and *S 109* (led by Leut-Commander Feldt) shattered the small convoy. At 0120 the Commodore's ship *Kongshaug* was torpedoed forward of the bridge on the starboard side. Already forty four years old the ship sank in 30 seconds. Commodore H Richman was struck on the head by a slab of concrete from the wheelhouse and had no clear idea what happened next. Whilst in the water he saw an engagement between the destroyer

Brocklesby (Lieutenant Commander E G Pumphrey DSO DSC RN) and an E boat before the destroyer picked him up. The *Pomella* was hit twice by torpedoes from *S 67* and abandoned. The *Reggestroom*, *Rosten* and the escort trawler *Manor* were missed from the convoy and presumed sunk.

The German air force now made its own contribution to the agony of WP 183. At 0610, when the remaining ships were south of Portland Bill, low flying aircraft swept in from the seaward side. The *Gripfast* was hit and sank at once. Survivors were picked up and gathered aboard the *Polly M* before being taken to Portland. Rescue operations mounted from Weymouth by *MGB 51* and *53*, *MTB 69, 87, 35* and *237*, searched widely for survivors and brought in twenty-eight men from the *Reggestroom*.

An enquiry was held into the disappearance of HM Trawler *Manor*. One survivor of the ship was picked up by HM Trawler *Ruby*, landed at Yarmouth, Isle of Wight and taken to Totland hospital. He was 2nd Hand Cyril Horace Joseph Foale. He recalled his experience, remembering that there was a tremendous explosion and the *Manor* settled by the stern. The force of the explosion flung the Commanding Officer and Cyril Foale backwards. The CO was flung back with considerable force and not seen again. Foale himself was caught up by the Asdic recorder which held him. Almost immediately there was a second explosion, and then a third that seemed to come from the forward messdeck. By this time the top bridge of the trawler was under the water and Foale began to float. Being a good swimmer he dived through a window, but on the way to the surface became entangled in the wireless aerial. He managed to get free and surfaced, holding onto a plank of wood until he found a lifebuoy. He shouted out in case there were any other survivors in the water, but there was no reply. Cyril Foale was the sole survivor. Though there would have been a number of ratings on deck at the time of the explosions, some manning the anti- aircraft guns and others on watch and at the wheel, none were seen again. The remainder of the ship's company was turned in below. The Carley floats were ready to be slipped and the lifeboat was slung out, but none of the watch below had time even to reach the deck before the little ship went down.

Through the winter of 1942/43 the convoys continued to make their way east and west along the English Channel coast. Often they spent one night at Portland, whereas previously they had only done so on rare occasions. Though the majority completed their journeys unscathed there were still fierce actions and losses. The Senior Escort, the Hunt class destroyer *Penylan*, fell victim to E boats while escorting PW 257 in December 1942. There were only seven merchantmen in the convoy, while the escort, in addition to the *Penylan*, consisted of trawlers and Fairmile Motor Launches. Convoy speed was six to seven knots, and the night of the attack was calm and dark with a light southerly breeze. Visibility was moderate to good. It was very cold. Early in the morning of 3 December Commander-in-Chief Plymouth informed the convoy that there were unidentified plots from Stoke to Prawle Point, but the captain of the *Penylan* was not informed. Later, tracks were plotted from Start Point to Bolt Head and it seemed clear that more than one group of E boats was present. The trawler *Ensay* obtained a hydrophone contact moving across the bow of the convoy. She fired star shells and saw a torpedo come from the port side and pass under her stern. At the same time a torpedo struck the *Penylan* amidships. The ship broke in half and sank within about fifteen minutes. The motor boat and whaler were destroyed in the explosion but Carley floats and other small life rafts were released and these helped the survivors to keep afloat. Some of the ship's company had kapok lined overalls which were meant for keeping warm as well as to serve as lifejackets. They were very effective.

Admiral Sir Charles Forbes, Commander-in-Chief Plymouth, commenting on the night's action, believed that the E boats should have been picked up by RDF. A convoy straggler may have caused confusion in RDF signals and the ship should have been made to catch up even if this meant sending an ML from the convoy escort. He also felt that HMS *Penylan* should not have been following a steady course at slow speed.

In February 1943, convoy WP 300 left Milford Haven, consisting of ten small ships and the larger Donaldson cargo vessel *Modavia* (5800 tons). The escorts, all manned by Norwegian crews, were a destroyer and two trawlers. The day after the convoy sailed, a reconnaissance aircraft flew over the convoy, whose progress was delayed when the whole group of ships turned back for a time to collect a straggler. At 0120 27 February, when off Berry Head proceeding at 9 knots, the *Modavia*, third ship in the starboard column, was torpedoed on the starboard side in No 4 hold. She sank at 0150.

In the same attack *LCT 381* was lost, and the Norwegian escort whaler *Harstadt* that had joined at Falmouth was torpedoed and blew up. The trawler HMS *Lord Hailsham* was also torpedoed right forward. She sank in two or three minutes. Some survivors managed to get aboard the trawler's sea boat while others, including Sub-Lieutenant John Makin RNVR, were able to release a Carley float. Eventually some sixteen men were picked up by the float which, though buoyant, floated low in the water so that the survivors were squatting in two feet of cold water. On seeing two large silhouettes against the night sky, the men thought they must be British destroyers out looking for them. Led by the Sub Lieutenant they broke

into a rendering of "Roll out the Barrel" until the shape of the ships or possibly the smell of diesel fuel made them realise that the vessels were in fact E boats sweeping the area to see what they could find. The survivors in the floats became quiet and still. The E boats moved away, apparently without seeing the men from the *Lord Hailsham*. At first light the survivors were picked up by MLs from Dartmouth and landed safely, though one had died of exposure during the night.

The E boats *S 65*, *S 68*, *S 81* and *S 85* of the 5th Flotilla were responsible for the successful German action.

On 9 February 1942, Vice Admiral Drummond had been replaced as Flag Officer in Charge, Portland, by Vice Admiral G T C P Swabey KBE CD DSO. George Thomas Carlisle Parker Swabey was born in 1881 and joined the Royal Navy in 1894. He was appointed Lieutenant in 1901, Commander in 1913 and Captain in 1918. In 1914, at the outbreak of the First World War, he was on board the battleship *Marlborough* on the personal staff of Vice Admiral Sir Lewis Bayly. He served as a Naval Observation Officer in the Dardanelles campaign and was awarded the DSO. His later service included the post of Captain of the Royal Naval College at Greenwich. He was a member of the New Zealand Navy Board from 1926 to 1929. He retired as Rear Admiral and was appointed Vice Admiral (Retd) in 1935. Recalled to service at the outbreak of war, he became a convoy commodore during 1940/1941, being torpedoed on one occasion. He served as Flag Officer-in-Charge at Portland until 1944.

7

THE SECOND WORLD WAR—TAKING THE OFFENSIVE

MGB 55 and other craft of the 4th MGB Flotilla alongside the pens at Portland. The Flotilla operated from Portland·and Weymouth during 1941-42.

HMS Attack, Operational Base for Coastal Forces

The presence of the Luftwaffe on French airfields and German E boats in the French Channel Ports determined the pattern of warfare in the English Channel. From the conquest of France in 1940 until the Allied invasion of Normandy in 1944, U boats did not enter the narrow waters. Instead, each side employed aircraft, light warships, and particularly coastal craft to attack and destroy enemy convoys and prevent shipping movements.

Britain began the war with two flotillas of coastal craft, one at Malta and the other at Hong Kong. There were also six Motor Anti-submarine Boats (MASB), while a small unit for working up was based at Portsmouth. There was a complete lack of experienced officers. Between the outbreak of war and April 1940, bases for Motor Torpedo Boats (MTB) were commissioned at HMS *Hornet* (Portsmouth) and HMS *Beehive* (Felixstowe). The urgent need for continued expansion led to the appointment of a Flag Officer, Coastal Forces, Rear Admiral P K Kekewich, who set up his headquarters at Portland in November 1940.

As one of a number of operational bases HMS *Attack* was commissioned at Portland on 15 January 1941, using the evacuated quarters of HMS *Osprey*. Flotillas soon began to arrive and by the middle of May the 4th Motor Gunboat (MGB) flotilla as well as the 4th and 5th Motor Launch (ML) flotillas were at the base. The 4th flotilla's *MGB 52* rescued Squadron Leader Blake of 234 Squadron RAF from the sea on the late evening of 9 July. The 4th ML flotilla was manned by Norwegians, and was visited by the Crown Prince of Norway in June. It was also in June that the 7th MGB flotilla arrived for work up, using American built boats acquired under Lend Lease arrangements. Two of these boats were unfortunately destroyed by fire on the late afternoon of 16 July. Working up and early operations were not without misadventures as the 5th MGB flotilla found when exercising at night and in fog during September. First of all *MGB 19* ran aground at Grove Point, Portland. When *MGB 17* tried to tow her off her propeller fouled the tow rope. It was the tug *Allen* that finally assisted the grounded vessel and she was successfully refloated. Meanwhile *MGB 18* had also run aground near Grove Point but she got off under her own power.

By January 1942, an anti-invasion force of coastal craft could be established, consisting of the eight boats of the 4th ML flotilla, four boats of the 20th ML flotilla and eight boats of the 4th MGB flotilla. Boats of the 11th MTB flotilla, some manned by Norwegians, took part in the Dieppe operation in August 1942 and were on a later occasion in action with German E boats. From 1941 until 1944 there were regular offensive and defensive patrols from HMS *Attack*, with the Portland boats sometimes joined by others from Newhaven.

The 63rd MTB flotilla was committed to defensive patrols off Portland during May 1944, losing two boats to attack from 'friendly' aircraft. Just after daylight on 5 May they were attacked by part of a formation of Beaufighters. *MTB 708* and *720*

both suffered damage and casualties from cannon fire and possibly from rocket projectiles as well. The planes attacked from ahead and then from astern. The MTB fired star cartridges when fire was opened on them and then replied with their own guns. *MTB 708* caught fire and the blaze spread throughout the boat. All firefighting equipment was destroyed and the boat was abandoned before being sunk by the destroyer *Cottesmore*. *MTB 720* returned to Portland with two main engines out of action, the third damaged and her fuel tanks punctured. Two officers and eight ratings were seriously wounded aboard the two boats and one officer and six ratings slightly hurt. Casualties from the boats were transferred from *MTB 720* to the frigate *Stayner* and later landed at Portland.

In the month preceding Operation Neptune the 1st Steam Gunboat (SGB) flotilla patrolled off Portland. Boats covered a combined exercise off Beachy Head during which *Grey Owl* and *Grey Wolf* were in action with E boats. Towards the end of May *Grey Fox*, *Grey Owl*, *Grey Wolf*, *Grey Seal* and *Grey Goose* crossed the channel on offensive patrol off the Channel Islands and the Cherbourg Peninsula. They were shelled by shore batteries and during the operation *Grey Owl* and *Grey Seal* collided. After a further offensive patrol in Seine Bay the flotilla sailed for Operation Neptune on 5 June.

As D day approached, the coastal forces flotillas moved into position to protect the assault convoys and prevent interference from enemy surface craft. The 2nd MGB flotilla and 63rd MTB flotilla were joined by the 7th and 25th ML flotillas, while two further flotillas of MTB joined HMS *Attack* in August and September.

As the land war moved eastwards and the German channel bases were overrun, so activity in the English Channel declined. HMS *Attack* continued to receive flotillas, however, even after VE day in May 1945. Though at first thinking that they might be sent to the Far East to fight the Japanese, the ships' companies in fact found themselves

The ML and Loading Jetties in 1944. MTB 701 forms part of the 63rd MTB Flotilla. ML 222 lies astern of her, while escort and supply vessels in the background occupy the length of the Coaling Pier.

Today a Channel Island ferry berth. In 1943 the jetties were occupied by Landing Craft and Coastal Forces attached to HMS BEE.

with little to do apart from a few exercises with frigates. The summer became idyllic after the rigours of war and the delights of Dorset beaches and Dorset pubs could be more readily enjoyed.

HMS Bee, Working Up Base for Coastal Forces at Weymouth

The growing strength of the Royal Navy in 1942 was demonstrated further by the establishment of a working up base for coastal forces at Weymouth. Training began in March, and in the first two weeks ten boats arrived and began their training programmes which lasted on average for five weeks. Commissioned as HMS *Bee*, the establishment was under the command of Commander R F B Swinley RN. Boats joining 'Swinley's Circus' were berthed alongside the north side of the harbour from opposite the theatre most of the way to the Town Bridge. They were camouflaged in a variety of schemes, blue and white, blue and grey, pale green and grey. One of them is remembered as being specially painted in irregular bands of sand, tan and pale green.

During the day, programmes were carried out at sea and ashore. Among the buildings occupied by HMS *Bee* was the Alexandra Gardens Theatre, half of which was made into a dining hall seating four hundred, while the other half was converted into a kitchen. Lectures were given in the Pavilion Theatre. Harbour drills included gunnery, torpedo and signals exercises. Navigational plotting exercises were carried out in a blacked out charthouse to simulate night action conditions. There was a radar workshop and an attack teacher. At sea, there were several exercise areas. The day might begin at 0830 and end after dark with small groups of boats engaged in manoeuvres and passing out exercises on completion of the work-up. A post mortem of each exercise was held in that part of the theatre set up as a lecture hall.

In December 1942 there were 26 craft working up at Weymouth and HMS *Bee* continued to operate vigorously throughout the year and well into 1943. By that time, plans were already afoot for the invasion of Europe and it became clear that the berths occupied by the coastal craft would soon be needed for another purpose. Landing craft and personnel

Coastal Forces craft attached to HMS BEE crowd the harbour at Weymouth in 1943.

would soon be needing accommodation for the assault planned for 1944. Weymouth, Poole and Portland would all be used to their full capacity.

The plan was that there would need to be accommodation for 28 major and 28 minor landing craft at Portland, 12 major and 36 minor landing craft at Weymouth, and 60 major and 10 minor landing craft at Poole. Most of the minor landing craft at Portland would be carried in LSI (Landing Ship Infantry). The headquarters for these activities would be in the buildings used by HMS *Bee*, for it was envisaged that Weymouth harbour would play an important part in the invasion operations, both in establishing a bridgehead on 'the far shore', and also in subsequent cross channel traffic.

The Commander-in-Chief, Portsmouth, Admiral Sir Charles Little, was loathe to transfer the training of coastal forces away from Weymouth, but he could see no alter-native. The Commanding Officer of HMS *Bee* in June 1943 was Captain E Pleydell-Bouverie RN. He wrote to the Commander-in-Chief and argued for the retention of the shore establishment by coastal forces, even suggesting that the port could become a permanent base for coastal force training, perhaps by the purchase of the outer portion of Weymouth harbour pier. Despite this spirited attempt to maintain *Bee* in its present location, Admiral Little still required the base to be moved as it would be needed by the landing craft in the middle of October. He was supported by the Assistant Chief of the Naval Staff (Home), who stated that the removal of *Bee* must be accepted, even though an alternative base at that time had not been found. 15 October 1943 was set as the change-over day. HMS *Bee* moved eventually to Holyhead and in its place HMS *Grasshopper* was commissioned at Weymouth to prepare for Operation Neptune.

8

COMBINED OPERATIONS

In 1940 and 1941 it was difficult to imagine any large scale operations from Britain against the French coast. But, particularly following the entry of the United States of America into the war in December 1941, the opportunities and resources for offensive action increased. The location of Portland and Weymouth Bay on the south coast of England meant that they were considerably involved in training for combined operations.

Group 2: *Garth* (destroyer), *Prinses Josephine Charlotte*, *Prinses Astrid* (Infantry Landing Ships), *MGB 316, SGB 6.*

Group 3: *Calpe, Fernie* (destroyers), *Glengyle, Prince Charles, Prince Leopold* (Infantry Landing Ships), *MGB 52, 57, ML 292, 281, 230.*

Combined operations forces exercised in Weymouth Bay in preparation for raids on Northern France in 1942.

By the summer of 1942 preparations were advanced for a raid on the French Channel coast. A combined exercise took place, code-named Exercise Yukon, leading to a practice landing on the beaches close to Bridport in Lyme Bay. Troop carrying ships assembled in three groups at Portland:

Group 1: *Albrighton (destroyer), Princess Beatrix, Prins Albert* (Infantry Landing Ships), *SGB 4.*

Five further groups of ships sailed from the Solent straight through to Bridport. More than thirty tanks were carried in LCT and a large contingent of Canadian troops made up the assault force.

A second exercise, Yukon II, planned for 22/23 June had as its objective:

... a raid on Bridport with limited air and military objectives, embracing the destruction of local defences and power stations and the capture of prisoners.

87

To achieve this it was planned that a force of infantry and tanks would land in the area of Bridport just before dawn and seize the town. The area would be held for some hours during daylight while various tasks were carried out. The force would then embark and return to its bases. The river gunboat *Locust* would provide supporting fire.

The Infantry Landing Ship *Prins Albert* came again to Weymouth Bay on 1 August and embarked troops of No 4 Commando for training under Lieut Colonel Lord Lovat. They had with them four United States Rangers. Practice landings were carried out at Lulworth, Worbarrow, and Osmington in Weymouth Bay. The *Prins Albert* was spotted by German aerial reconnaissance on 8 August, following which efforts were made to disguise the ship as a merchantman and she was moved into Portland harbour alongside the coaling pier. These preparations were for the raid on Dieppe, Operation Jubilee, that took place on 19 August. Though the Commandos were successful in their attack on the German battery at Varengeville, the main assault was bloodily repulsed with heavy losses to the Canadian troops and the tanks that got ashore.

During 1943 experimental work was carried out in waterproofing armoured cars for landing from assault craft. In April *LST 301* experimented with 150 ft vehicle landing ramps. Further exercises with Canadian troops were carried out at the end of the year under the codename Exercise Vidi, assaults being made by 8th Infantry Brigade and No 7 Beach Group on beaches at Studland. Under the overall command of Commander R E D Ryder VC, troops boarded their transport ships at Portland, including the *Lady of Man, Victoria, Brigadier, Invicta, Canterbury, Duke of Wellington* and *Mecklenberg*. Other vessels assembled at Poole, Stokes Bay and in Southampton Water. The realism of these exercises was assured by the use of live ammunition in machine guns and covering fire.

By 1944 detailed planning for Operation Overlord was well advanced. A conference was called at the Naval Centre, Portland, on 9 February 1944 'to cover the provision of accommodation for assault forces during the assembly for Overlord'. It was planned that there would be a total of eleven flotillas of landing craft of various kinds at Portland and nine flotillas at Weymouth. It was no doubt intended that the assault forces comprising the British Force G would load and set out for France from Dorset ports. The decision, however, to increase the strength of the initial assault by landing on more beaches caused a revision of plans. In April 1944 Force G received its final berthing orders and moved to the West Solent, Southampton, Beaulieu River, the Hamble and Yarmouth. The bases at Weymouth and Portland were reallocated to the United States Force 'O', destined to land on Omaha Beach .

Already US troops had arrived in Britain in large numbers and were engaged in assault training. Among the beaches used for their practice assault was Slapton Sands in South Devon.

At 0220 on the morning of 28 April a telephone call alerted British and United States forces at Portland that a disaster had hit Convoy T4, composed of Landing Ships Tank (LST) engaged in manoeuvres off South Devon. The eight LST in the convoy were attacked by nine E boats of the 5th and 9th Flotillas some twelve miles from Portland Bill. The weather was fine with little or no moon. The convoy was under the close escort of a single corvette, HMS *Azalea*. The destroyer *Scimitar* should also have been with the convoy but she had been rammed by the United States *LCI (L) 324* and holed on the port side of the forecastle above the waterline. The damage meant that the ship was seaworthy only in calm waters. Failure of communication led to the Operations Officer at Plymouth being totally unaware that *Scimitar* had not sailed or been replaced by another ship. As soon as the error was discovered, the destroyer *Saladin*, a sister ship of *Scimitar*, sailed from Start Bay at 0137. But she was too late.

The LST were moving ahead in line at 3½ knots, preceded by *Azalea*. At 0215 the rear LST was torpedoed, followed immediately by another. *Azalea* zigzagged among the now scattering LST but saw no E boat and feared to fire star shells lest she expose the vulnerable landing craft to further attack. In the sharp action *LST 507* and *531* were sunk. *LST 289* was severely damaged astern and was escorted to Dartmouth. All were crowded with American assault troops.

Covering forces reached the scene of the disaster quickly. The destroyers *Obedient* and *Offa* arrived first and made contact with the E boats but were unable to engage them. From 0500 to 0700 the *Onslow*, *Obedient*, *Brissenden*, *Saladin* and *Azalea* picked up survivors. During the morning 291 survivors were landed at Portland including those brought in by *LST 515* and *511* of the assault convoy, and some fifty ambulances were engaged in ferrying survivors to hospitals even as far away as Sherborne. Casualties however were heavy. During the next few days, small naval vessels returned from patrol carrying the bodies of victims of the action. It was estimated that some 320 bodies were recovered. Many of the soldiers who had drowned were wearing their lifebelts round their stomachs instead of under their armpits and this had forced their faces down into the water.

The Exploits of MTB 344

Coastal forces vessels were used to carry out combined operations on the enemy coast. In particular the record of one small ship is worthy of note. *MTB 344* was an experimental boat built by Thornycroft at Hampton with two Thornycroft engines plus a Ford V8 auxiliary which could be clutched into the starboard shaft for silent running. Lieutenant F W P Bourne RNVR was appointed to command the boat on 27 July 1942 and was attached to the Small Scale Raiding Force (SSRF) while nominally part of the 11th MTB Flotilla based at HMS *Hornet* at Gosport. From that time until May 1942, Lieutenant Bourne carried out some 17 operations.

The SSRF was based at Anderson Manor, near Bere Regis in Dorset. In August 1942 *MTB 344* first went to Portland and took on board Commandos for night exercises. Once she became operational, she awaited her first signal to be at Portland or Dartmouth for a particular operation. Some 24 hours in advance of the operation Lieutenant Bourne would meet the leaders of the raiding force, and then the motor torpedo boat would be prepared for the operation.

Although originally fitted with two 18 inch torpedo tubes, these were removed when the boat was required for combined operations.

MTB 344 at speed off the English Channel coast. She is carrying troops of the Small Scale Raiding Force as well as her naval complement.

Her armament was 2 Lewis guns, two .303 Vickers guns, two depth charges and smoke making apparatus. To land the raiding force an 18 foot Dory was carried, hauled up on a ramp over the stern by a hand winch. The crew of one officer, one coxswain, one motor mechanic and one stoker, a wireless operator and three seamen all used a small mess deck forward. At first the boat was camouflaged in a sea green colour, but later Lieutenant Bourne changed this to Mountbatten pink as it was more effective at night. Once all the necessary checks had been carried out, the boat fuelled and the dory prepared for silent operation, it only remained to work out course and speeds from the point of departure to the anchoring position off the enemy coast. Information on the location of minefields and German E boats was obtained from naval intelligence. Accurate navigation was essential to the success of these operations, and to aid the MTB's commanding officer, a Belgian, Lieutenant Rick Van Riel sailed on operations with particular responsibility for tidal and navigational details. Known as 'Vann', Van Riel had already had an exciting war, first in escaping from Dunkirk and then operating in enemy territory during the summer of 1940. Finally the party of up to 12 Commandos would arrive on board *MTB 344* and disperse themselves about the boat.

From the autumn of 1942 through to the Spring of 1943 the raiding parties sailed, usually at dusk, to cross the English Channel to France or the Channel Islands, carried out an operation and returned at dawn. Many of these voyages began and ended at Portland. Risks were high and success often elusive. In adverse weather conditions *MTB 344* was not an easy boat to handle, being difficult to manoeuvre in high winds.

Operation Dryad, carried out in September 1942, was successful. The intention was to land on the Casquets Isle and take prisoners. *MTB 344* had engine trouble on the outward voyage that reduced her speed; nevertheless the early stages were completed at 25 knots, later increased to 33 knots. The raiding party

was put ashore and succeeded in capturing seven prisoners including two leading telegraphists. They all re-embarked and were back at Portland at 0400.

A few days later *MTB 344* sailed again for the island of Burhou to see if it was occupied and if it was possible to land pack artillery there. Again there was engine trouble, this time with the port engine, but the outward passage was completed and the anchor dropped at 0015. Captain Ogden Smith, 2nd Lieutenant Lassen and six other ranks landed on the island. No inhabitants were found and a survey of the island showed that it would be possible to land pack artillery there. While the party was ashore, watch was kept on lights and signals from the Casquets and Alderney. The return passage was completed at 0430.

On 3 October Operation Basalt took the little ship to Sark, leaving Portland at 1903 and returning the next morning at 0633. Five Germans were found, four of whom were killed while attempting to escape. The fifth prisoner, from the Pioneer Corps, had been engaged in mining the beaches.

Operation Batman took place on 15 November 1942 with the object of landing a raiding party on the Cherbourg peninsula and taking prisoners. *MTB 344* sailed at 2145 with a party of officers and men of the SSRF. The night was cold and completely overcast. Visibility was never good and reduced to half a mile in coastal fog. Nevertheless the passage was made at 28 knots until the Alderney light was seen and landfall made on the French coast at 0016. Visibility continued to be poor, especially after the moon set at 0050. Rocks could only be picked out at a cable. It was not until 0125 that the ship's position was known for certain and the Pointe du Nez identified.

Time was now against the operation for it would have taken the MTB another hour travelling at silent speed to get to a landing position, and by that time she would have been close inshore for more than two hours. A flashing light had been seen and it was possible that the ship had been detected. When a breeze sprang up from the north, producing a short, choppy sea, it was decided to abandon the operation and *MTB 344* turned for home. She entered Portland harbour at 0422 having encountered no other ship during the entire voyage.

A landing was planned for December 1942 in which *MTB 344* would carry only 4 SSRF men, two of whom were to land on one of the Sept Isles. For this operation, codenamed Fathom, the motor torpedo boat was to sail from Dartmouth but would return to Portland by 0815. Her orders on returning to England were specific:

> *MTB 344* is not to approach the English coast during the dark hours except in an emergency when she is to make every effort to establish her identity with coast defences, breaking W/T silence only if the situation demands.

A planned raid on St Peter Port in Guernsey never took place. Operation Witticism, to be led by Lt Commander R P Hichens DSO DSC RNVR with *MGB 111* and *112* was postponed in December 1942. Another attempt was made in January with *MGB 112* only, but once more weather conditions turned against the venture, this time only after the force had been at sea for more than two hours.

Operation Huckaback was successful on the night of 27/28 February 1943 when *MTB 344*, once more engaged, transported a raiding party to Herm. No enemy opposition was encountered.

The risks of this kind of raid were demonstrated once more in Operation Backchat, when on 1 March 1943, *MTB 344* took a party of the SSRF to reconnoitre the beach at Anse de St Martin on the Cherbourg peninsula. As the MTB manoeuvred in the area at 2330 two searchlights were switched on over a mile away and guns fired shrapnel that burst 150 ft in the air. Two small ships, possibly patrol vessels, were seen. As the enemy seemed to be on the alert it was decided to abandon the operation and the MTB returned to Portland at 0200, presumably taking good care not to be mistaken for an E boat by the coastal defences.

Following this operation it seems that *MTB 344* did no further work from Portland. She had gone for overhaul in January 1943 after six months or more continuous work. She was later attached to the 1st Flotilla, went to Northam for refit before rejoining at Newhaven, from which base she carried out more operations. From July 1943 until July 1944 she was commanded by Temporary Sub Lieut J F Russell-Smith. While at Newhaven

COURTESY J.F. RUSSELL-SMITH

Lieutenant Van Riel (extreme left), navigator aboard MTB 344 with Temporary Sub Lieutenant J.F. Russell-Smith. Note the emblems on the bridge screen.

she was struck astern by a torpedo accidentally fired from *MTB 252*, and her commission ended on 12 July 1944 when she was paid off for disposal.

These clandestine operations, testing the enemy's defences and seeking vital information for the future invasion of France across the Channel, were carried out with skill and determination. Though on occasion criticised, the navigational skills of the CO of *MTB 344* and of Lieut Van Riel were tested to the full, and the bravery of the men in the boat's crew and in the raiding parties must be recognised. They were not, however, reckless, recognising that to slip away quietly and return another night was far more worth while in the long run than to tempt fate with a landing when the enemy was already alert or when the weather conditions in the English Channel put the success of an operation at risk.

9

THE SECOND WORLD WAR—D DAY TO VE DAY

D Day and After

The decision to use Portland and Weymouth as departure ports for the United States 1st Division was followed rapidly by detailed instructions and action. As a result of a conference with Vice Admiral Swabey and his Chief of Staff, Captain Sandford RN, Captain J J McGlynn USN recommended that all three Portland hards should be operated by the US Navy, that HMS *Grasshopper*, the Royal Navy base at Weymouth after the departure of HMS *Bee*, should be taken over by the US Navy and operated as a landing pier for Infantry Landing Craft (LCI(L)), and that officer space, quarters and messing facilities, together with space for the installation of repair and maintenance facilities, should be allotted to US forces.

Captain McGlynn took up his post as Commanding Officer USNAAB (United States Navy Advanced Amphibious Base), Portland and Weymouth, on 16 April 1944 and the base itself was formally commissioned on 1 May. Personnel were transferred from Teignmouth and Appledore, while the bulk of the administrative personnel and 'hard' crews came from USS *Milwaukee,* a cruiser that had just previously been transferred to the Soviet Navy. When the 'hard' crews arrived, they had in fact never seen a hard before. The tests of the efficiency of these men came with Exercise Fabius, scheduled for three days from 29 April. It was during this exercise that the landing craft were attacked by E Boats off the South Devon coast.

The naval commander of Force 'O', Rear Admiral J L Hall USN arrived at Portland

Shipping in Portland harbour shortly before D-day 1944. The headquarters ship USS ANCON and three assault transport are visible together with LCT and LCI.

aboard the headquarters ship USS *Ancon* on 29 April, together with the first assault transport ships *Samuel Chase*, *Charles Carroll*, *Anne Arundel* and seven destroyers. From that day until 5 June, ships steadily assembled in Weymouth Bay and in Weymouth and Portland harbours. Not all the ships were American. The transports that were to take the US Rangers to their assault on Pointe du Hoc included the British manned *Ben-My-Chree*, *Prince Charles*, *Prince Leopold*, *Princess Maud* and *Amsterdam*. The British ships *Empire Anvil* and *Empire Javelin* carried United States Army assault troops as did the US transports *Henrico*, *Thomas Jefferson*, *Dorothea L Dix* and *Thurston*.

The orders for the US forces were set out in a communication dated 8 May 1944:

1. In the forthcoming operation the US naval commitment will be the Western Task Force comprised of Assault Forces 'O' and 'U' and follow up force 'B'. These forces will be predominantly American with British units attached: ships and craft of almost all classes will be included.
2. It is planned that Portland will serve as the principal base for Force 'O' during the assault and follow up and subsequent build up. Units of the control force and Force 'U' will also base there.
3. The mission of US Naval Advanced Amphibious Base, Portland-Weymouth will be to:
   a. prepare, assemble, maintain and provide logistic support for US naval forces based there.
   b. carry out the naval phase of loading of military and naval forces in accordance with operational orders.
   c. sail ships and craft in accordance with operational orders.
   d. receive US ships and craft for unloading of survivors, casualties, prisoners etc.
   e. operate with FOIC, Portland, TURCO* in the build up.

The Flag Officer-in-Charge, Portland, received orders detailing the task of his sub command. He was responsible for:

1. necessary sailings for assembly of Operation Neptune.
2. co-operation with Senior Naval Officer, Bombardon-Mulberry Project.
3. co-operation with Forces 'O', 'U', 'B' sailing for the assault and follow up.
4. co-operation and control of covering forces of the 'Western wall' with the Commanders-in-Chief, Plymouth and Portsmouth.
5. escorting and sailing build up convoys and landing craft as in operational orders.
6. arrangements for Air Sea Rescue.
7. protecting ships in Portland harbour, Weymouth harbour and Weymouth Bay.

May was a month of intense activity. Headquarters were set up ashore for LST and LCT flotillas. Lieutenant Commander John D Bulkeley USN set up a base for American motor torpedo boats, known as PT boats, a force that grew to a strength of three squadrons. On 25 May King George VI, with Admiral Sir Bertram Ramsey RN, Commander-in-Chief of Operation Neptune, the sea borne side of the invasion, Rear Admiral Alan K Kirk USN and Rear Admiral J L Hall USN inspected the landing craft and took a trip in a PT boat through the ships and craft assembled in Portland harbour. The period was described as one of "back breaking toil, meticulous checking and tension".

It was a constant source of astonishment to service and civilian personnel in the area that the German Air Force made no serious attempt to interfere with the massive build up of naval and military forces prior to the launch of Operation Neptune. Such attacks as did occur took place at night. Light raids were carried out on 20, 24 April and 7, 14, 15 May, but it was not until 28 May that any serious disruption was caused to the build up.

On the night of 28 May, some thirty German planes flew over Portland under the cover of returning RAF bombers. They dropped flares, then bombs fell on Portland and Weymouth, and mines were laid in Portland harbour. The harbour was already full of ships and craft preparing for the assault. A number of landing craft were damaged by

---

*TURCO—Turn Round and Clearance Organisation.

Landing craft load from the Portland hards as part of the US invasion force, June 1944. 3 LCT are in the foreground. Behind them, more LCT and the larger LST are awaiting for the order to depart.

underwater explosions. Fortunately, accurate plots were made of eight parachute mines through the organisation led by Lieutenant C A Oliver RNVR, the mine spotting officer. Immediately the raids ended the Senior Officers of 104 and 167 Minesweeping Flotillas were ordered to clear the mines. Portland harbour was closed all day to shipping and movements within the harbour were stopped. One American launch ignored this order and detonated an acoustic mine; fortunately both members of the crew were saved. *MMS 74* touched off two mines and *MMS 279* got a third. During the day, seven of the eight parachute mines were accounted for. The eighth, it was later confirmed, had drifted across Chesil Beach into West Bay. The port was then re-opened and embarkation for D day was resumed.

The US Infantry came to Weymouth in trucks from their camps. They debussed at Greenhill, close to the shore. Pausing at a stall serving coffee and doughnuts they then marched along the Esplanade to board the landing craft that waited for them in the harbour. Tanks and vehicles forming the assault and follow up forces, moved south along prescribed routes down through Wyke Regis to the narrow bridge joining Chesil Beach and Portland to the mainland. They then moved to assembly points where they were grouped by the craft load and in turn reversed aboard the waiting landing ships and craft. Each vessel took about half an hour to load with its vehicles. A total of 501 ships and craft were berthed and loaded at Portland and Weymouth before D day.

As early as January 1944 the harbour at Portland had been laid out with ten trots of seven buoys apiece to receive the LCT. As the ships received their loads of tanks, guns, trucks, men and equipment, they moved away from the landing stages and loading hards to tie up to the mooring buoys. There, with all personnel sealed in, they awaited their orders to depart for the far shore.

All was ready for the original D day of 5 June. But a postponement for 24 hours due to

bad weather made matters very difficult for the Portland sub-command. The weather began to worsen on 3 June and the signal ordering the postponement was made at 0515 4 June. Two United States groups of landing craft that had sailed from Devon and Cornwall did not apparently receive this signal and early on the morning of 4 June were already 25 miles south of St Catherine's Point and still steering for France. The sloop HMS *Hind* was ordered from patrol at 0805 to contact the convoys, and later a Walrus aircraft from Warmwell, a US destroyer and HMS *Campbell* managed to turn the 200 craft of groups U2A1 and U2A2 towards Weymouth Bay. Although 50 craft had reached the shelter of the bay by noon, the majority did not arrive until 2200 when they had to sail again for the new D day on 6 June. Furthermore these craft had to be clear in time to enable the vessels of Force 'O', already at Weymouth and Portland, to sail on time. That this was more or less achieved was a tribute to the initiative, discipline and organisation of those involved.

The intense activity can be imagined. The headquarters ship *Ancon*, the landing ships for infantry, the landing craft for tanks and personnel, the escort ships, and the minesweepers all prepared to sail according to their orders. The old French battleship *Courbet* was towed from the bay towards her final resting place as a blockship to the Mulberry harbour. At 1630, the monitor HMS *Erebus*, with the destroyer USS *Gherardi* ahead of her as screen, sailed for her bombardment position off the Normandy coast. At 1730, the powerful bombarding force to support the landing at Omaha beach, had the Portland Bill lighthouse abeam. The battleships USS *Texas*, *Arkansas* and *Nevada*, the French cruisers *Georges Leygues* and *Montcalm*, USS *Tuscaloosa* and *Quincy*, HMS *Glasgow*, *Bellona*, *Enterprise*, *Hawkins* and *Black Prince*, with their escorting destroyers, steamed eastwards up channel towards 'The Slot', the great swept channel leading from the Isle of Wight towards the beaches.

United States LST loading supplies at Castletown, Portland, 2 June 1944.

As the vessels sailed out of Weymouth Bay, they could hear and see overhead the aircraft and gliders of the airborne troops making their last landfall at Portland Bill before heading for their dropping zones. By midnight the harbours were almost empty, save for local craft and the fast motor torpedo boats that were scheduled to make passage at dawn. After the intensity of the preparation, all that those on shore could do was to wait and hope that the operation would succeed, that soon they would be sending supplies and troops to support and follow up on the landings, and that not too many casualties would be coming back in the returning ships as witness to some disaster on the far shore.

The troops that sailed from Portland and Weymouth that day, though they did not know it, were to face the most fiercely contested landing of the whole operation. They headed for Omaha beach.

The headquarters ship USS *Ancon* anchored 13 miles off Omaha beach at 0251 6 June. Though the severe weather of the previous days had improved, the wind still gusted strongly and the waves varied between three and six feet. Assault landing craft were launched and the specially prepared DD tanks, designed to 'swim' ashore, began their long and in most cases disastrous journey towards the beaches. Leading troops of the 116 and 16 Infantry Regiments with beach landing teams approached the shore to find that the beaches were unscarred by air bombardment. Liberators of the United States Eighth Air Force had been forced to bomb through cloud and their loads had exploded from 1000 yards to three miles inland from the shore. Waiting for the American troops to touch down were the German 726th Regiment and three regiments of the front line 352nd Division. The hail of fire that greeted the attacking infantry caused heavy casualties and for a time it seemed probable that the attack would be thrown back into the sea. As the infantry struggled to get off the exposed beaches, two Ranger battalions attacked the gun emplacements at Pointe du Hoc by climbing the cliffs against fierce German opposition.

Among the assault troops was the novelist Ernest Hemingway, reporting on the invasion. He sailed across from Portland in the troopship *Dorothea Dix*, while the war photographer Robert Capa crossed in the *Samuel Chase*. Hemingway's vivid account is one of the best descriptions of the landings,* while Capa's photographs, one hundred and six of them, might have been the best photographs of the invasion, had not all but eight negatives been destroyed by an accident in the darkroom.

At last the invading troops wore down the opposition and began to move inland. Empty landing ships and craft returned to England to reload with build up troops and materials. Some of these returning ships carried the first casualties of the assault. At first there was difficulty in dealing quickly with the craft returning to Portland, particularly those carrying wounded men. One LST arrived at Portland harbour with 88 casualties, including 6 critically wounded men. She reached the harbour at 1100 on D+3. She was not called into the hard until 24 hours later and none of the wounded was removed until the ship reached the hard, even though the CO had reported that he had six critical cases on board. Later the removal of the wounded became more efficient with particular commendation being given to the kindly and sympathetic attitude of the American coloured litter bearers.

Following D day, ships continued to cross from Portland to the far shore until 27 April 1945 when the last LST sailed for France. Large naval and air forces were assigned to the protection of these ships and their precious cargoes against German aircraft, surface forces and U-boats. It was to be expected that there would be casualties on both sides.

Before the month of June 1944 had passed, the escort groups patrolling the channel to the west of the landings had destroyed two

*Colliers Magazine 22 July 1944, also in By-Line (Penguin 1970).

Landing craft, trawlers, drifters and Motor Gunboats assembled at Portland before D-day, June 1944.

U-boats in the Portland area. The frigates HMS *Affleck* and *Balfour* sank *U 1191* off Portland Bill on 24 June and the next day HMS *Bickerton* destroyed *U 269* in the same area. The *Bickerton* left her group to land survivors and while the remaining ships of the escort group, HMS *Keats, Goodson, Bligh* and *Aylmer* were cruising in line abreast and zigzagging at 15 knots, the *Goodson* was hit aft by an acoustic torpedo fired by *U 984*. The *Bligh* took *Goodson* in tow and headed for Portland. The ships stopped to allow a convoy to pass. While stopped the rolling of the ship caused a large piece of the *Goodson's* stern to break off and sink. Yawing increased but at 2250 the tug *Pilot* came alongside, the *Bligh* slipped her tow and the *Goodson* was

The destroyer was at defence stations with all Oerlikon guns and pompoms manned in addition to part of the main armament. All hatches were battened down and mess decks cleared. The ship was zigzagging at about 9 knots. There were many aircraft in the vicinity when, at about 0445 a Junkers Ju 88 torpedo carrying bomber attacked the destroyer from the port bow. The identification of a hostile aircraft was not made until it was too late to take avoiding action. The German plane launched two torpedoes, one of which exploded in the wake of the *Boadicea*. The other hit the forward magazine which blew up with such force that the ship forward of the engine room disintegrated into a mass of twisted steel from which there could be no

The destroyer BOADICEA was escorting a convoy off Portland on 13 June 1944, when an aerial torpedo detonated her forward magazine.

brought alongside the coaling wharf. Casualties were sent to the 50th Field Hospital.

One week after D day, 13 June, the destroyer *Boadicea* was sunk by aerial torpedo. The *Boadicea* was stationed 2000 yards ahead of convoy EBC 8 of 13 ships sailing eastwards in two columns at about 6 knots.

survivors. The after part sank very rapidly, certainly in less than three minutes. Of the ship's company there were only twelve survivors, two officers and ten ratings being taken aboard the destroyer *Vanquisher* and landed at Portland.

The Board of Enquiry under Captain C C Sandford of HMS *Boscawen* attached no blame to the Commanding officer, nor any of the ship's company of the *Boadicea*. Difficulties in aircraft identification were recognised, particularly when a number of RAF Beaufighters had been seen with their navigation lights on, aeroplanes similar in outline to the Junkers Ju 88.

Two days later the frigate *Blackwood* (Lt Cdr L T Sly RD RNR) was torpedoed and sunk by *U 764*. The *Blackwood* was part of the 3rd Escort Group. At 1911, when steaming at 12 knots, there was a violent explosion and a dense cloud of yellow smoke hid the ship from view. When the smoke cleared it could be seen that the whole of the forepart of the ship had been blown away, the mast had collapsed and the bridge structure had been flattened back. The *Blackwood* did not sink at once, but it was clear that she must be abandoned. Two Air Sea Rescue launches *HSL 2696* and *HSL 2697*, manned by RAF personnel, saw the explosion and went to the rescue at full speed. They took survivors aboard, assisted by the frigate *Essington*. Temporary Surgeon Lieutenant M J Brosnan RNVR aboard the *Blackwood*, described in vivid terms what occurred when the ship was hit.

At 1900 hours on the 15th June I was sitting on the settee in the wardroom. One of the stewards was laying the table for supper. We were at Cruising Stations and so far as I know nothing out of the ordinary was going on. The sea was calm with a slight choppy wave but no swell and the ship was perfectly steady . . . About 1905 the phone buzzer rang. Lieutenant Johnson, the Navigating Officer, answered it and left the wardroom. He told me later that the Captain had sent for him.

About a minute later there was a blinding flash, a bang and the sound of tearing metal. On coming to, I was lying in the corner under a piece of the wardroom table. The wardroom was full of wreckage and water was pouring over everything. I managed to crawl out and made for an open space thinking that the ship was going down. My senses had partly returned by this time and I saw that the water was coming down from above. I became conscious of a lot of white smoke and a strong

smell of cordite. Everything was dead quiet except for the sound of running water. The engines appeared to have stopped. The forward end of the wardroom and all forward of this was blown away. The port side of the wardroom with the cabin leading off were also missing. The plates on the port side were all blown outwards and I climbed round them and got onto the deck further aft. Two bodies were hanging over these plates with blood pouring out of them and were obviously dead.

I then went aft. The deck was littered with debris and in this I saw a three inch projectile which I threw overboard. The binnacle of the gyro compass was lying just outside the galley. Two ratings were lying on the deck in the waist. I examined them but both were dead. Another rating was lying near the depth charge racks. He had multiple fractures of the arms and legs and was also dead.

I then met several stokers and ordered them to go forward and look for wounded people which they did. The Sick Berth Attendant then appeared. He gave me a first aid bag and a supply of morphia. We did not know then how long the ship would stay afloat or if we might not get torpedoed again: so the SBA and myself decided to have everything in readiness for abandoning ship as soon as possible or for transferring to another ship, which might come alongside. I did not carry any wounded below decks for these reasons. We agreed that as the SBA was uninjured and could climb, he should concentrate on getting all the wounded down from the bridge and upper decks and bring them aft where I would attend to them. This he did with the help of some stretcher bearers. The more seriously wounded cases were laid down on blankets on the deck in the spaces on either side of the Bofors director housing. They had some protection from the cold evening wind, which had sprung up. It was found to be impracticable to carry stretchers into the after heads on account of the right angle bends. The less severely wounded and walking cases, however, were able to shelter here. Most of the injuries were either head injuries or broken limbs. They were all cold, shocked and soaking wet and thoroughly miserable. I gave morphia to all those without head injury and wrapped them well up in blankets which I had brought up from below. Extra splints, slings and bandages were brought up from the Sick Bay. The only lights below were too small portable hand lamps which came on automatically

The First Lieutenant was carried aft quite early. He was injured in the back, head and arm and was semi-conscious. He had been found on the Boat Deck between the Oerlikon guns. I was informed that the Captain was lying seriously wounded on the bridge and that the SBA was attending to him. I saw Sub-Lieutenant Renny standing on the deck and asked him if he was all right. He did not reply but stared vacantly in front of him. His face and clothes were black and filthy. He did not appear to be bodily injured so I told a rating to put a blanket around him and take him out of the cold. I later saw him on one of the launches but he did not appear to recognise me or be capable of thinking.

I also saw Lieutenant Johnson twice. He was standing at the waist both times and appeared to be in a similar state to Sub-Lieutenant Renny, but was able to say "I am all right Doc." in a very weak voice. He refused to lie down and gave me the impression that he felt that there was something which he should do but couldn't remember what it was. I asked him had anything been done about the Confidential Books and told him to try and find these and also any valuable instruments. A short time after it struck me that perhaps he had not comprehended what I had said to him. So I told a rating to try and find them.

I asked an ERA if the engines could be restarted and the pumps got going but he said he did not think so. So I sent him to find the Chief ERA (I had already been told that the Chief Engineer and four other officers were missing—also the Chief Stoker). I did not see the Chief ERA at any time and as I was fully occupied with my medical duties I concluded that the engines could not be re-started and left it at that. I do know that the forward Engine Room was flooded and that the forward Motor Room must have been damaged as there was a large hump 1½ to 2 feet high on the deck just above this room and the whole ship was raised at bow and stern. A search party was sent down into the Seamen's mess deck under the Wardroom. It was flooded and full of wreckage. Two injured ratings were got out but the remainder were floating about and were either dead or drowned. One rating was

trapped and after a lot of trouble he was released but unfortunately was also dead.

The hatches leading down to the forward Motor Room were jammed shut and required crowbars to open them before the occupants could be got out. They were uninjured. At about 2000 hours two Air Sea Rescue launches made fast alongside the starboard side. The wounded were transferred to these as quickly as possible. The more serious cases were put into one of the launches. It was my intention to go ashore with these cases, while the SBA looked after the less serious cases on the other launch. While this was going on the uninjured ratings collected their kits and then got onto the launch with the less seriously wounded.

About this time I saw a Motor Boat from one of the other ships come up to the stern. I did not receive any instructions from them and they left again after a few minutes. I noticed a ship standing off about a quarter of a mile away.

Shortly before we left the ship the SBA managed to lower the Captain from the bridge onto the forward launch. This was a very difficult and lengthy job as the Captain is a very heavy man and was severely wounded and in great pain; and also all ladders had been blown away. He also lowered the Asdic rating down on a piece of ladder after this. Unfortunately this rating died on the way in. (These two were the only persons left remaining on the bridge after the explosion.) I consider that the SBA did a very fine job and is deserving of full credit for it. He showed great initiative and devotion to duty under difficult circumstances.

At about 2100 everybody was off the ship except for the SBA and two ratings whom I sent back on board to search for any injured or trapped still remaining who might have been overlooked. The dead had already been carried down to the mess deck and the hatches closed. I did not give any orders to abandonship, but thought it advisable as I concluded that they were waiting until we were all off before putting salvage party on board and taking the ship in tow.

Shortly afterwards both launches left the ship. She then had a slight list to starboard and the deck forward was about 3'6" from the water while aft the transom was out of the water with about half of the propellers and rudders showing. The launch went across to HMS *Essington* and when about 30 yards away somebody shouted down from the bridge "Do you want anything from the Sick Bay, Doctor." I was standing on the bows of the launch at the time attending to an injured rating and replied "No, I am all right now thank you." Something else was said but I did not hear what it was.

Three ratings died on the launch on the way in. They all had severe head and other injuries. There were no deaths on the other launch. Between the two launches there were about 100 survivors and of these about 35 were wounded."

Towards the end of June, Major General Collins' Seventh Corps in Normandy was approaching Cherbourg. The capture of the port was essential to the build up of Operation Overlord. A Task Force was assembled by Rear Admiral Deyo to bombard the German batteries defending the port. There were two bombardment groups:

Bombardment Group One: cruisers USS *Tuscaloosa* (SO) and *Quincy*, HMS *Glasgow* and *Enterprise*; battleship USS *Nevada*; six destroyers.

Bombardment Group Two: battleships USS

HMS GLASGOW is hit twice by shells from German shore batteries defending Cherbourg. The GLASGOW landed her wounded at Portland.

IMPERIAL WAR MUSEUM

The *Blackwood* remained afloat throughout the night, but at 0410 16 June, as the *Duckworth* and *Domett*, joined by the *Braithwaite* from Portland, closed the wrecked ship, radar contact was lost as she sank out of sight.

The Air Sea Rescue launches, which now included *HSL 2691*, and carrying the survivors, reached Portland just before midnight.

Texas (Flagship) and *Arkansas*; three destroyers.

A force of minesweepers would sweep a channel for the bombarding ships. The 9th and 159th Minesweeping Flotillas of the Royal Navy together with eight US Navy minesweepers made up this force.

The ships sailed from Portland at 0430 25

June and by midday were in position. They opened fire and bombarded targets east and west of Cherbourg. Two hundred rounds were fired by the bombardment groups which in turn came under accurate return fire from the German guns. The cruiser *Glasgow* was hit twice and the Captain and Commander of the *Enterprise* were wounded by splinters from shells that fell 50 yards on the port side of the ship. Personnel at Portland were warned that the battleship *Texas*, returning to the harbour, had an unexploded 240mm shell on board in the warrant officers' accommodation. Bomb disposal men removed the shell, transferred it to a small boat and defused it. By 1930 ships of the force were back at Portland except for the

Vice-Admiral R.J.R. Scott. Flag Officer, Portland from October 1944 to July 1945.

Enterprise which sailed for Portsmouth. The *Glasgow* discharged ten ratings to the Royal Naval Hospital.

A further bombarding force left from Portland in August when the battleship *Rodney* sailed to shell a German battery of four 305mm guns on the island of Alderney.

Instructions by letter ordered the *Rodney:*
a. to inflict as much damage as possible on the enemy.
b. to investigate what damage could be expected from the deliberate bombardment by a capital ship at long range.

Optimum conditions were required. The ship was not to sail from Portland until the RAF confirmed that weather conditions were satisfactory. She also had to sail to the bombardment position and back in the same day. To give controlled conditions *Rodney* was to anchor and use in the main, single 16 inch guns. Tugs would be available to keep the ship in position, preferably with her bows pointing westwards towards the target.

On 12 August conditions favoured the operation and the *Rodney* sailed at 0730 with the destroyers *Jervis* and *Faulknor*. The battleship anchored off Raz de Bannes beacon at 1243. At 1412 the main armament opened fire across Capde la Hague. In all 'A' turret fired 25 rounds from one gun, 'B' turret fired 50 rounds, 19 from one gun and 31 from another, while 'C' turret, masked from the target by the position of the ship, fired no rounds at all. Firing was completed at 1644, and *Rodney* was back at Portland by 2212. It was reported that the first 16 inch shell fell on a farmhouse, but the rest of the shoot was accurate. Spotter aircraft reported that hits were made on three of the four gun emplacements.

Vice Admiral Swabey was replaced by Rear Admiral R J R Scott as Flag Officer-in-Charge, Portland, from October 1944 to July 1945. Richard James Rodney Scott was born in April 1887. By 1911 he was in the Royal Navy and serving in the submarine depot ship *Rosario* at Hong Kong. At the outbreak of war in 1914 he was aboard the *Hecla* a depot ship for torpedo boats and destroyers. During the war he served overseas in the cruiser *Talbot* and by early 1919 had attained the rank of Acting Commander aboard her. In March 1919 he was appointed to command the sloop *Myrtle* which, with the *Gentian*, was mined on 16 July 1919 whilst operating against the Bolsheviks in the Gulf of Finland.

COURTESY A. SCOTT

For his bravery after the mine struck the vessel, he was awarded the Albert Medal. Between the wars he served aboard the sloop *Carnation* and the cruiser *Dauntless*. He attended the Staff Course in 1925 and was then appointed to the Training and Staff Division. Following service aboard the battleship *Ramillies* he became Captain of HMS *Queen Elizabeth*. In 1939 he was Director of the Royal Naval College Greenwich before taking command of the 11th Cruiser Squadron. During the Second World War he served as Flag Officer-in -Charge, Iceland, from 1940 until he became Rear Admiral (Training) in South Africa in 1942.

It was only after the landings in Normandy in 1944 that German U-boats made any serious attempt to disrupt convoy traffic in the English Channel. They did not succeed and suffered heavily in the attempt. But they had some successes. The passenger ship *Leopoldville* (11,500 tons) was sunk by *U 486* north of Cherbourg while on passage from Spithead in convoy WEP 3. She was lost on Christmas Eve. As the year came to an end, *U 772*, on what was to be its final patrol, attacked convoy TBC 1 off Portland Bill.

The convoy was in two columns of ten ships with the corvette HMS *Dahlia* ahead and HMCS *Calgary* on the port beam. *U 772* attacked from astern, firing torpedoes that hit the American merchantmen *Arthur Sewall* and *Black Hawk*. The *Arthur Sewall* first to be hit, was struck in the engine room, pulled out of line and stopped. The *Black Hawk*, rear ship of the starboard column, was torpedoed aft. *Dahlia* and *Calgary* hunted the attacking U-boat, the latter dropping depth charges. By this time the 21st Escort Group appeared on the scene and the two convoy escorts returned to their

U 249 arrives in Weymouth Bay on 10 May 1945 having accepted unconditional surrender.

charges. A number of survivors were picked up by the *Dahlia* who proceeded with them to Brixham. The *Calgary* escorted the remainder of the convoy, *Arthur Sewall* struggled into Weymouth Bay and dropped anchor, while *Black Hawk* was beached further east in Worbarrow Bay with her stern blown off. *MTBs 750* and *760* from Portland were ordered to search for survivors. They approached the *Black Hawk* and, on hailing her, heard a whistle and found a Chinaman on board, badly injured on a platform in the after hold and surrounded by oil and water.

In the early hours of the next morning, while moving submerged with her schnorkel extended, *U 772* was spotted by a Wellington IV aircraft of 407 Squadron RCAF, on patrol from Chivenor. The Wellington, after one pass, swept round to attack again and dropped an accurate pattern of six depth charges close to the schnorkel. The U-boat was not seen or heard of again.

With the dawn of 1945, victory for the Allies was clearly in sight, though it was certain that it would not easily be won. The land battles of western Europe had moved far to the east of Normandy, but still an average of five LST left daily from Portland for the far shore. The last sailing was on 27 April. Danger to the ships from surface vessels and aircraft may have passed but the risk of U-boat attack remained. Escort groups and other ships in the western Channel frequently reported suspected contacts and sometimes attacked them with depth charges. Often it became clear that the contact was almost certainly a wreck. Nevertheless ss *Everleigh* was torpedoed and sunk by *U 1017* on 6 February

when she became a straggler from a convoy. 43 members of her crew were taken aboard *LCI 33* and landed at Portland. Six men were lost and of the survivors 14 were admitted to the Royal Naval Hospital.

Minesweepers from Portland began the clearance of mines. A mined area south of the Shambles was cleared successfully in January and work began in Lyme Bay. Ships of 135 Group of Motor Minesweepers were engaged in this work.

By April the European war was drawing rapidly to a close and during the month exercises took place in connection with the anti-submarine defences of Portland. These were carried out by the midget submarine *XT2*. Other special trials with torpedoes involved *MTB 109*.

The order for U-boats to surrender brought three submarines into Weymouth Bay. At 0922 9 May Oberleutnant Kock in *U 249* surfaced in the Channel and offered to surrender. The frigates HMS *Magpie* and *Amethyst* were ordered to intercept and bring the submarine into Weymouth Bay. They arrived on the morning of 10 May. Unconditional surrender was accepted and the 5 officers and 43 ratings of *U 249* were removed from the U-boat as prisoners of war. On the same day *U 1023* was brought in. *U 776*, having surrendered, was escorted into the bay by the frigates HMS *Garlies* and *Gore* on 16 May. While she was at Portland, surface trials of special radar equipment were carried out aboard *U 249*, and before the end of May *U 776* sailed for London and *U 1023* for Plymouth. The European war was over.

10

PEACE WITH VIGILANCE

AUTHOR'S COLLECTION

Returning after war service in the Pacific, the battleships NELSON and QUEEN ELIZABETH came to Portland in 1946.

Home Fleet and Training Squadron

Portland returned to its peacetime role. With the end of the European war, naval attention was turned towards the Pacific and the Far East where American and British forces were building up to conclude the conflict with Japan. The atomic bombs on Hiroshima and Nagasaki largely persuaded the Japanese to surrender and by the autumn of 1945 the Second World War had ended.

Though the pressure for demobilisation at the end of the war could not be resisted, it was decided to retain compulsory National Service at least for the time being. Long term plans were presented for the development of a fleet no longer dominated by the concept of a big gun battle fleet, but more concerned with task forces centred upon aircraft carriers, and on the maintenance of an anti-submarine capability. The original plans, outside the scope of this work, had to be cut again and again in response to economic pressure and changed perceptions of the role of the fleet in hot and cold war, in Europe, the

North Atlantic and the Third World. The Korean War, for example, showed that the weak British economy could not sustain service development programmes and the civilian export trade while at the same meeting the sudden demands of a rearmament programme. If Britiain was to survive economically, then the cost of defence could not be permitted to restrict economic growth. Activities at Portland reflected the changes in strategy and tactics. Though at first these changes were observed through the conversion of existing ships to their new roles, later years saw the arrival of new designs of warship and aircraft incorporating advances in electronics and weaponry.

The anti-submarine school, having left Portland during the Battle of Britain in 1940, returned from Largs in March 1946, and in the same month the Home Fleet sailed on its first peacetime Spring cruise since 1939. In size this fleet bore no resemblance to the mighty squadrons that had assembled before the war. One battleship, the *Nelson*, and

The Open Cutter Race 1948 with the aircraft carrier VICTORIOUS of the Portland Training Squadron in the background.

two cruisers, *Birmingham* and *Diadem* with their accompanying destroyers, sailed under the flag of Vice Admiral Sir Edward Syfret. Later in the year the battleship *King George V* arrived at Portland escorted by the destroyers *Escapade, Easton, Obdurate, Offa* and the frigate *Helmsdale*. Excercises and trials programmes began. It was during calibration trials that the tug *Buccaneer* was sunk by a shell from the destroyer *St James*.

The tug was struck by a 4.5 inch shell under the rubbing strake at the after end of the engine room, while another shell plunged close to the counter. Lieutenant Commander S E Veal MBE RN (Retd) commanding *Buccaneer*, ordered that a collision mat be placed over the hole but this failed to check the inrush of water. At the same time the loss of steam prevented the effective use of the ship's salvage pump. The *St James* (Commander J Lee-Barker DSO RN) whose B turret had fired the fatal shot, closed *Buccaneer* and went alongside to take off the crew. This was achieved successfully but 25 minutes after being hit the tug went down, damaging the destroyer's starboard propeller as she did so.

Portland's post war role in the training of Royal Navy personnel began with the establishment of the Portland Training Squadron, at first known as the Battleship Training Squadron. In succeeding years the battleships *Nelson, King George V, Anson* and *Howe* and later the aircraft carriers *Victorious, Illustrious, Implacable* and *Indefatigable* took their turn as part of the training squadron. Classrooms were built in the hangar space of *Victorious* and extra beds were fitted. Training was provided for new entry ratings and basic training was given for short service aviation cadets. On occasion, units of the Training Squadron accompanied the Home Fleet on its Spring Cruise. In the years immediately after the war there were problems in manning the ships while rapid demobilisation took place. When units of the Home Fleet assembled at Portland in January 1947, Rear Admiral H Hickling CBE DSO, commanding the Battleship Training Squadron, stated in a speech at Dorchester that only by drafting sailors to the Home Fleet from the Training Squadron was it possible for there to be a Spring Cruise at all. At that time there were three battleships under his command—*Nelson, Anson* and *Howe*.

An important series of trials in refuelling at sea (RAS) were carried out in 1947 between the *Bulawayo*, a fleet replenishment ship, and the battleship, *Duke of York*, the cruiser *Superb* and the destroyer *Dunkirk*. The tests took place in good weather conditions between Portland and the Isle of Wight. No difficulty was encountered in refuelling with the ships abeam of each other at 12 knots steering into the wind, or

The cruiser SUPERB was part of the Home Fleet in the years immediately after the war.

at 15, 18 and 20 knots steering with the wind astern. It was found that, if the warship approached the tanker from the quarter, this caused areas of pressure resulting in loss of propulsion. A better approach was to come abeam of the tanker at a distance of half to one cable and then edge into the refuelling station. The only limiting factor seemed to be the amount of water coming aboard while refuelling in bad weather. The tests included refuelling while ships were turning, refuelling by the astern method, night RAS and the transfer of heavy stores.

The battleship *Duke of York*, flying the flag of Admiral Sir Roderick McGrigor, sailed from Portland on the 1948 Spring cruise, and in June her sister ship *Anson* embarked the Duke of Edinburgh and Princess Elizabeth for a visit to Guernsey. The battleship was escorted by the destroyers *Wizard* and *Roebuck* and four motor torpedo boats. At the end of the month Exercise Verity, involving British, French and Dutch warships began off Penzance and finished at Weymouth on 7 July. The battleship *Anson* took part in the exercise with the aircraft carriers *Implacable*, *Victorious* and *Theseus*, the French aircraft carrier *Arromanches*, the cruisers HMS *Superb*, HMS *Cleopatra*, *Georges Leygues*, *Montcalm*, *Gloire*, *Tromp* and destroyers, escorts and submarines.

Tragedy befell a motor pinnace carrying fifty one liberty men back to the aircraft carrier *Illustrious* on the night of 17 October 1948. The ship was in harbour as part of the Training Squadron. The weather was rough when the pinnace left Weymouth harbour just after 2200. On leaving the lee of the breakwater to enter Portland harbour, the boat was steered into a head sea and foundered only fifty yards from the *Illustrious*. Twenty nine men were drowned including Midshipman R A Clough, the officer in charge of the boat. The pinnace should not have been carrying more than forty men and should have turned back on entering the rougher water. At a Board of Enquiry Midshipman Clough was held to be responsible for the accident. His parents suggested to the Admiralty that their son may well have been exhausted by the long hours of duty over the previous weeks. The Board of Enquiry was reconvened, and friends of Midshipman Clough, while not denying the arduous nature of duty, reckoned that he had been fit, well and in good spirits. It was clear from the Captain of the *Illustrious* that the ship had had a very busy commission that had taxed the ship's company, causing them in the words of the enquiry report "to want to run before they could walk". Sixteen of the men drowned in the accident are buried in the cemetery above the naval base.

A more balanced force than hitherto was assembled for the 1949 Spring cruise, when Admiral McGrigor's flagship was joined by

Libertymen from the aircraft carrier INDEFATIGABLE and the battleship VANGUARD coming ashore at Weymouth.

the aircraft carrier *Theseus*, four cruisers and a number of destroyers. During the cruise to Gibraltar a helicopter was carried to deliver dispatches between ships.

The flagship of Admiral Sir Philip Vian on the 1950 Spring cruise was the aircraft carrier *Implacable*. The battleship *Vanguard*, together with the aircraft carrier *Illustrious* joined the fleet. The *Vanguard* was the last British battleship to be built. She formed part of the Training Squadron at Portland from November 1949, though she temporarily flew the flag of the Commander-in-Chief Home Fleet for the Autumn cruise of 1950 and the Spring Cruise of 1951. She was the flagship of the Training Squadron until she left for refit in September 1951.

The aircraft carriers *Theseus* and *Ocean* were fitted out for service in the Training Squadron in 1954, replacing *Indefatigable* and *Implacable*. By 1956 over 4,000 officers and ratings had been trained annually with the squadron. All seamen passed through as did National Service officers. In times of emergency the carriers could be diverted from their training role. In

the crisis in Cyprus, for example, they were used to carry military vehicles to the island.

The state of the national economy prevented the navy from sending its big ships on long cruises. Though much training was carried out in harbour, the ships did take part in Home Fleet exercises. It was sometimes said that Chief Petty Officers and Petty Officer Instructors disliked the posting partly because of the absence of sea time. But within three years, the smaller size of the operational fleet required that ships' companies should be efficient even before they joined their squadrons. It was therefore decided to appoint a Flag Officer Sea Training, the first appointment being made in April 1959. This officer was responsible for the organisation and control of the working up in home waters of cruisers, destroyers and frigates. He was also to advise on the suitability of shore and sea training to the needs of the fleet, and on complements provided for the operation and maintenance of cruisers, destroyers and frigates. He flew his flag at Portland naval base, and still does so.

HMS VANGUARD, the last British battleship in commission, came to Portland in November 1949 as a training ship. She later became flagship of the Home Fleet.

measuring 24 feet by 28 feet. As a result of the trials Bristow recommended that an automatic mooring device should be developed and that a turntable could prevent damage to the rotor blades of the helicopter when on the deck of a ship. Further operational experience was gained when a helicopter accompanied an Antarctic whaling expedition. Helicopters were soon in use tracking homing torpedoes from destroyers, while the possibility of working from the decks of merchant ships was considered.

In November 1946, Captain R J Shaw RN of HMS *Osprey* submitted a paper entitled 'Tactical Employment of Anti-Submarine Helicopters'. Shaw believed that the most important attributes of helicopters were in an anti-submarine role. Their extreme flexi-

An historic photograph . . . A Hoverfly seen in company with a King George V class Battleship in 1946.

Helicopters and The Fleet Air Arm

Perhaps the most significant developments witnessed from Portland in the immediate post war period were those concerned with the Fleet Air Arm and helicopters. At first, experiments were conducted with helicopters in relation to work with the fleet. Tests were carried out to see if they could land on small ships, how they handled, how they coped with the rise and fall of the deck and how they might survive exposure to the elements. Sikorski R4B Hoverfly aircraft were used and fitted with 'balloon bag' undercarriages. The first landing onto a frigate was made by Lieutenant (A) A Bristow RNVR of 771 Squadron on 6 September 1946. He landed on the frigate *Helmsdale* which had been specially fitted with a wooden platform

The original small ships flight deck. The wooden planking of HMS HELMSDALE. Lieut. Alan Bristow (later to become Chairman of his own international helicopter company) lands on . . .

The frigate HMS HELMSDALE served at Portland after the war as a trials ship. The photograph shows the first landing of a helicopter on the deck of a small warship in September 1946. From such small beginnings . . .

bility and mobility compared favourably with anti-submarine vessels. They could maintain close and accurate contact with a submarine once located, and they were available as immediate air reinforcements under the control of the Screen Commander. Shaw also assumed that some form of helicopter direction would be fitted in anti-submarine warships.

The ability of the helicopter to travel fast to a given spot and then to hover made it particularly suitable for investigating possible contacts at a distance from the close escort or screen. Furthermore a submarine may be lured into a false sense of security and be led to an incautious use of high submerged speed. Alternatively, the suspected presence of a helicopter could force a submarine to make frequent use of periscope or radar and so forfeit mobility.

Captain Shaw concluded that there were three important functions in anti-submarine work that helicopters could perform. They could augment the Close Surface Escort, investigate contacts at a distance and act as contact keeper. Limitations would be imposed by maintenance and endurance, both of machines and personnel.

The Director of the Joint Anti-submarine school at Londonderry recommended that trials should continue using the Hoverfly

flight to develop techniques and elementary tactics using estimated data for Asdic performance, or by fitting the helicopter with expendable towed sonar buoys. Tactical investigations might be carried out at *Osprey* and the Joint Anti-Submarine School, again using estimated data.

The Admiralty responded on 14 July 1947: Their Lordships are of the opinion that . . . no useful purpose would be served in making use of the Hoverfly for anti-submarine trials at sea pending the availability of British helicopters designed for operational employment, and are anxious that the employment of the few Hoverfly that are available should be limited to more or less essential services to conserve maintenance spares.

During the bitter winter of 1947 the King, Queen and the Princesses Elizabeth and Margaret sailed in the battleship *Vanguard* to visit South Africa. The destroyer *Offa* sailed from Portland to form local escort to the battleship. Despite the adverse weather conditions, Lieutenant Kenneth Reed and Lieutenant-Commander R Parkinson flew from Portland in a Sikorski Hoverfly and made the first landing of a helicopter on the quarter deck of a battleship when they set down on the *Vanguard*.

Fleet requirements work continued with helicopters during the 1950s, but it was not until 1959 that the Royal Naval Air Station, Portland, was commissioned as a helicopter base for anti-submarine warfare machines in training with submarines and escort vessels. In 1961 No 771 Helicopter Training and Trials Squadron was commissioned at Portland under Lieutenant Commander A I R Shaw MBE AFRAeS RN. It was equipped with Wessex, Whirlwind, Dragonfly and P 531 (prototype Wasp) machines. In July a P 531 suffered a tail rotor failure and crashed into the sea. One member of the crew was killed and the other rescued by the frigate *Troubridge*.

Portland waters were witness to development in fixed wing aircraft for the Royal Navy. It was in bright sunshine in the early afternoon of 8 February 1963 that the aircraft carrier *Ark Royal* was steering east off Portland Bill at 5 knots. Down from the sky came the Hawker P 1127 prototype VTOL—Vertical Take-off and Landing aircraft piloted by Hawker's chief test pilot, A A Bedford. The aircraft flew past *Ark Royal* at 400 knots and then turned to make the first vertical landing by a fixed wing aircraft on the deck of an aircraft carrier.

On the last day of April 1985, the author witnessed the arrival of five Sea Harriers to land aboard the aircraft carrier *Illustrious* as she steamed across Weymouth Bay. In succession the jets flew alongside the carrier, hovering opposite the selected landing position on the ship before easing over the flight deck and landing. The whole operation of landing on was completed in a few minutes.

HMS OSPREY

HMS DARK GLADIATOR—a fast target ship at Portland in the sixties—carries out a personnel transfer with a Wessex MK1.

DAYS NEVER TO BE REPEATED

The last days of the "big ship" fleet assemblies . . .

Naval Base Modernisation

Dockyard works were carried out to adapt the base to the changing roles required of it. In 1946 the six 55 ton cranes on the coaling pier were dismantled. Each was brought to the point of balance with wedges, then pulled into the coaling pit by a mobile crane. New heavier capacity cranes were installed. The coaling pit was in part built over at a later stage and partly used for storing gear. Eight Phoenix units were brought to Portland from the wartime Mulberry harbour and located to the west of the berths and jetties as a protection against the prevailing westerly winds. It is believed that six of these Phoenix units were sent to Holland in 1953 to counter the severe flooding that had occurred.

In the early fifties berthing facilities for warships were improved by building a new,

600 yard long, deep water jetty to the west of the existing berths. A large area was reclaimed from the sea by driving sheet piles into the harbour bed and filling in behind them with quarry waste. For the new pier itself, known as Queen's Pier or Q Pier, concrete piles were made on site. More than five hundred were constructed, floated on pontoons into position and then driven into place with steam hammers. An eighteen inch thick reinforced concrete jetty was built. Finally, the old destroyer pens that had served for fifty years were broken up.

Until 1959 there was a floating dock at Portland. In the early 1920s there was a large floating dock in the harbour and the chart for 1926 shows a floating dock located between the Coaling Pier and the Dock Jetty. In August 1940 the trawler HMS *Hertfordshire* was in dock when it was

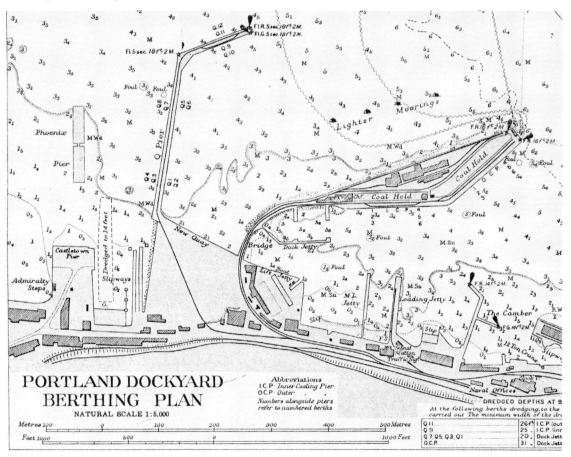

PORTLAND DOCKYARD
BERTHING PLAN
NATURAL SCALE 1:5,000

Abbreviations
I.C.P. *Inner Coaling Pier*
O.C.P. *Outer*

Numbers alongside piers refer to numbered berths

The building of Q pier, in the background the Phoenix units from the Mulberry Harbour can be seen in position.

damaged, holed and strained. The ship was extricated without further damage. After the war floating dock AFD 19 enabled repairs and refits to be carried out without the delay of sending ships to dock facilities elsewhere. Submarines, the frigate *Helmsdale* and at least one Blackwood class frigate are known to have entered the dock.

The coaling pier was adapted and partly built over by the contractor A E Farr Ltd. More land was reclaimed to build and extend the helicopter base, and a building programme has continued throughout the seventies and eighties to provide for a busy naval base.

On any day at the time of writing, a number of British, Dutch, German and Belgian ships may be seen working up under the Flag Officer Sea Training (FOST). Methods of training devised and developed since 1961 are employed to test each ship at the beginning of a commission. Weapons, efficiency, machinery, tactics, organisation and performance are subject to rigorous scrutiny. Complex threats are introduced to provide a conflict of priorities and every man in a ship's company is

One more steam cranes return to Portland . . . to help build the new Q pier.

The frigate HEDINGHAM CASTLE in dry dock at Portland, July 1947.

The coal has gone . . . but the name remains. A new jetty is built over the existing coaling pier. A Type 14 frigate and RFA TIDEFLOW can also be seen.

By 1971, additional land had been reclaimed and a base for helicopters had been established.

involved. The Admiral and his staff embark to advise, observe and analyse a ship's performance. They will also inject incidents without warning. The author observed the rapid response aboard a Belgian frigate, which, while refuelling at sea, was suddenly presented with the situation 'Man overboard!' Several ships are involved at a time and they exercise with Royal Fleet Auxiliary tankers and replenishment ships. The ships are subject to attacks by submarines, surface vessels and high speed passes by jet aircraft from the RNAS, Yeovilton. Exercises are as real as possible and include refuelling at sea, damage control, and landing parties for riot control in support of civil authorities. Each exercise is followed by a thorough review—"washing up!"

Weymouth. The destroyers *Meredith* and *Hawkins* came in June 1950 while in July 1952 the giant battleship *Missouri* of 45,000 tons, the cruisers *Macon* and *Des Moines*, together with their destroyer escorts, anchored in Portland harbour. Two months later the 51,000 ton aircraft carrier *F D Roosevelt* anchored in Weymouth Bay.

The establishment of the North Atlantic Treaty Organisation and the presence of the Flag Officer Sea Training at Portland brought many NATO warships to the base; this continues right up to the present time. The Standing Naval Force Atlantic (Stanavforlant) was inaugurated at Portland on 13 January 1968 "to threaten no-one, but to help keep the peace and dissuade any potential troublemaker in the vital area of the

The US heavy cruiser USS DES MOINES at Portland 1952.

The long tradition of visits by foreign warships continued after the war. The US cruiser *Helena* visited Portland in March 1946 supported by the destroyers *Cone* and *Glennon*. Indeed United States warships were at first the most frequent visitors. The cruiser *Fresno* and the destroyer *Zellars* in 1947 were followed by the visit of the cruiser *Spokane* in December that year as part of the ceremony of the unveiling of the D day memorial on the Esplanade at

North Atlantic." The force comprised between four and eight destroyers and frigates. The first Commodore, Captain G C Mitchell RN had under his command the Royal Navy frigate *Brighton*, the Dutch *Holland*, the Norwegian *Narvik* and the United States destroyer *Holder*. These ships were later joined by the Canadian escort *Gatineau* and the West German frigate *Koln*. Ships of the Standing Naval Force have visited Portland frequently since.

Submarines

The suitability of the English Channel for submarines and anti-submarine exercises meant that submarines continued to operate from Portland as they had before the war. The large submarine depot ship *Maidstone* was a familiar sight in the harbour with submarines alongside her. She continued the tradition set by earlier depot ships, *Vulcan*, *Titania* and *Alecto*, but she had the added distinction of flying the flag of the Commander-in-Chief Home Fleet from September 1956 until March 1958. She was equipped as a parent ship for submarines, with a foundry, light and heavy machine shops, and electrical and repair shops. She had facilities for recharging submarines' batteries and in addition to her own armament, mounted a four inch gun on a submarine type mounting for training submarine gun crews. There were carpenters' shops and plumbers' shops. Facilities for submarine crews included a laundry, hospital, chapel, canteens, a bakery and a barber's shop. After service at Portland the *Maidstone* went to Portsmouth from 1958 to 1962 for reconstruction as a support ship for nuclear submarines.

Maidstone lay at a permanent mooring buoy, her bows pointing to the west. Submarines came alongside her in trots both on the port and starboard sides. On occasion a practice torpedo might be fired from alongside. Aviation cadets went aboard to visit submarines and even school parties sometimes toured the ship.

Building upon recent experience of submarine warfare, submarines sought to travel longer distances under water, and at greater submerged speeds. Torpedoes were further developed using new fuels. The submarine *Tudor* returned to Portland in September 1947 from a 3,800 mile scientific expedition into the eastern Atlantic. Two months later the *Turpin*, *Trump*, *Tradewind*, *Tactician*, *Tiptoe*, *Taurus* and *Sanguine*, ships of the 2nd and 5th submarine flotillas, exercised with *Maidstone* and the destroyer *Opportune*.

Tragically the submarine *Affray* was lost in April 1951 after sailing from Portsmouth. Portland based ships joined in the search being conducted by Captain M J Evans in the destroyer *Agincourt*. Four frigates, *Tintagel Castle*, *Flint Castle*, *Hedingham Castle* and *Helmsdale* sailed at once as well as the submarines *Seadevil*, *Scorcher* and *Sirdar*. But the position of the missing submarine was not known and it was only after a search lasting two months that the *Affray* was finally located by sonar, lying in some 228 feet of water about 30 miles north of Guernsey. The Type 162 sonar, developed at Portland and designed to detect submarines and wrecks, was instrumental in finding the missing submarine. The submarine *Sidon* actually spent five hours on the sea bed 27 miles south of Portland Bill while ships passed over her, testing Asdic gear in conditions similar to those in which *Affray* might have been lost.

HMS *Sidon's* log records typical submarine activity at Portland. She often came to harbour stations at 0800, courses and speeds for leaving harbour were established, and by about 0930 the submarine would be well out to sea. She would then dive, probably to 30 feet and exercise with surface ships, sometimes one ship in the morning and another in the afternoon. She would then return to harbour in the early evening. During a typical month the submarine would dive to different depths, perhaps carry out bottoming trials, full power trials, and practise man overboard and gun action. Anti-submarine exercises with British and American destroyers and frigates were frequent, and occasionally a mock attack would be carried out against another submarine. While alongside the depot ship, hands were employed 'in compartments, to make and mend clothes, and in cleaning ship.'

The *Sidon* herself was victim of an explosion four years later. On the morning of 16 June 1955 she was preparing to sail on exercises to test "fancy SR" torpedoes using a new fuel, high test peroxide. With the British submarine *Subtle* and the Danish submarine

H Class submarines—seen here alongside their depot ship HMS ALECTO—operated with the anti-submarine flotilla in the training role.

HMS TITANIA with her brood of H and R class submarines.

HMS MAIDSTONE was a familiar sight at her mooring close to the naval base in the 1950's. In the background are three research vessels which were moored in the harbour for many years.

HMS TINTAGEL CASTLE. Ships of the Castle class were based at Portland for many years as Training ships. They took part in the search for the missing submarine AFFRAY.

Saelen the *Sidon* lay alongside the depot ship *Maidstone*. Two experimental torpedoes were embarked aboard *Sidon*. One of them was perfectly sound, but fuel began to flow from the other after it had been placed in the torpedo tube and the doors shut. Tremendous pressure built up. At 0845 an explosion blew off both doors with most of the pressure passing rearwards into the submarine. A sheet of flame was seen to shoot up through the conning tower, followed by another that flung furniture and pieces of clothing into the air. The fuel in one of the test torpedoes had ignited. *Sidon* listed and began to settle.

Temporary Lieutenant Charles Eric Rhodes was among the first to enter the submarine after the explosion. Despite smoke and darkness he succeeded in bringing an injured man to safety. He then put on a Davis Submarine Escape apparatus and went back into the submarine to aid the injured. He helped two more men to escape before the submarine finally sank. Surgeon Lieutenant Rhodes was not a submarine officer. He was not familiar with the layout of the submarine nor was he experienced in the use of the escape breathing apparatus he had put on. Even so he had no hesitation in entering the submarine to give medical aid. He did not survive, but died of asphyxiation after trying unsuccessfully to climb through the conning tower. For his bravery he was posthumously awarded the Albert Medal. Two other officers and ten ratings from *Sidon* were killed.

The salvage vessel *Kinbrace* sailed from Dover and *Barcross* set out from Portsmouth. The work of salvage began. By means of camels and cylinders, the submarine was lifted and beached close to the oil tanks on the western side of the harbour. It was one week

HMS BARCROSS uses camels to raise the submarine SIDON before beaching her.

The US nuclear submarine NAUTILUS coming alongside on the completion of her record breaking voyage.

after the explosion. *Sidon* did not return to service. Two years almost to the day after the tragedy she was towed out of Portland harbour and sunk in 20 fathoms as a sea target. The date was 14 June 1957.

The world's first nuclear powered submarine, the USS *Nautilus* visited Portland in 1957 and 1958. On the first occasion, in October 1957, the submarine berthed alongside the depot ship USS *Fulton*, well away from shipping, and the public could not visit her. British naval officers and technicians were allowed on board to inspect the submarine, and the First Sea Lord, Admiral of the Fleet Lord Louis Mountbatten, brought Duncan Sandys, then Minister of Defence, on a visit. Negotiations were taking place with

the United States government for the provision of American propulsion machinery in the first British nuclear submarine to be built, the *Dreadnought*.

Under her commanding officer, Commander W R Anderson USN, the *Nautilus* came to Portland again on 10 August 1958. On this occasion, she arrived having sailed from Honolulu and passed submerged under the polar ice, reaching the North Pole on 3 August. Coming alongside Q pier, Commander Anderson and his ship's company were given a rousing welcome on their achievement.

An explosion aboard the submarine *Alliance* on 29 September 1971 killed one man and injured thirteen.

RFA BLACK RANGER—very much part of the Portland scene. She conducted countless refueling exercises with ships working up in local waters.

The Ocean going tug SEA GIANT . . . one of many PAS (later RMAS) craft to perform vital target towing and berthing duties around the naval base.

The Second Frigate Squadron

Ships of the Second Frigate Squadron, with a red 2 on their funnels, became 'day runners' from Portland. They joined with submarines, and helicopters from Osprey, in exercises to give training with anti-submarine sonar and helicopter landing control. They also gave practical training at sea for newly joined ratings. The squadron was led by the frigate *Undaunted* which was built as a 'U' class destroyer and completed in March 1944. After active service in operations off the coast of Norway, she took part in Operation Neptune and on D+2 she carried General Eisenhower, Allied Supreme Commander, on a tour of the beaches. Before the end of the war the *Undaunted* had served in the Western Approaches and with the British Pacific Fleet. In 1952 she was converted into a type 15 anti-submarine frigate. The conversion was not completed until 1954 when she joined the Second Training Squadron as a trials ship. From 1962 until she finally paid off the *Undaunted* was a familiar sight at Portland. The squadron was commanded successively by Captain A D Cassidi, Captain B C G Hutchins, Captain J B Robathan and finally Captain R M Burgoyne. Of the remaining ships in the Second Frigate Squadron at Portland some were Type 14 frigates, including the *Dundas, Hardy, Russell, Palliser* and *Exmouth*. This last ship was also a trials ship for a gas turbine propulsion system. Other ships in the squadron acted as trials ships. The *Verulam* was converted for experimental work in anti-submarine detection, followed by the destroyer *Matapan* whose conversion completely transformed her appearance. The *Grenville* and *Penelope* were also trials ships and *Ulster* worked with the squadron out of Portsmouth.

The squadron was not entirely confined to Portland waters, making two visits a year to north west European ports. In 1971 for example, the frigates *Undaunted, Ulster, Grenville, Hardy, Dundas* and *Palliser* with *RFA Grey Rover* exercised in the area of Jutland and German Bight before visiting Copenhagen.

The commissioning of the Royal Naval Air Station in 1959 as part of HMS *Osprey* demonstrated that the shore establishment was becoming more concerned with the role of the helicopter in anti-submarine warfare.

HMS DUNDAS. Type 14 frigates replaced the Castle class at Portland and were seen operating from the base for twenty years.

The frigate UNDAUNTED as leader of the Second Frigate Squadron

Research, Development and Espionage

The post war period saw a progressive increase in the research and development programmes in underwater warfare at Portland. The Anti-Submarine Experimental Establishment of 1946 was followed by the Underwater Detection Establishment from 1947 to 1962. Work in underwater weapon research was combined in 1962 with the formation of the Admiralty Underwater Weapons Establishment, Portland (AUWE); and the Admiralty Gunnery Establishment buildings were taken over at the southern end of the island. The AUWE was renamed the Admiralty Research Establishment (ARE) in 1984.

centrate underwater weapon research there. This led to the test and evaluation of equipment produced in Western Europe, Canada and the United States of America. From 1956 onwards, work progressed on homing torpedoes and other under sea missiles. Mine warfare was also an important part of the establishment's work.

It was not surprising that the secret nature of most of this work attracted the attention of the Soviet Union. The post war development of the Russian Fleet as a world wide ocean going navy, together with its massive production of submarines, formed a major threat to Britain and her allies. Anti-submarine

CROWN COPYRIGHT

The last of the World War 2 Hunt class. HMS BROCKLESBY was reprieved from the breakers and served at Portland as a seagoing test bed for experimental anti-submarine devices being developed ashore.

To a large extent the work of the research establishments continued that of HMS *Osprey* between the wars. Asdic, now called sonar, was developed further. The effective range of sets was increased, and it was said that by 1960 the range could be as much as 75 miles. The sounds of the reactor in a nuclear vessel could be identified and the possibilities of long range underwater search by radio beam were investigated. Variable depth sonar buoys were produced as well as aerial sonar for use by the growing number of anti-submarine helicopters. Work at Portland was further enhanced by the NATO decision to con-

measures amongst the NATO navies would be of primary concern to Soviet Intelligence.

It was in the climate of the cold war that the Portland spy case came about in 1961. It was discovered that Harry Frederick Houghton, who had served in the Royal Navy for more than 22 years, was passing information to Russian agents in the persons of Gordon Lonsdale and the Krugers. Houghton was at that time a clerk employed by the Ministry of Defence at the Port Auxiliary Repair Unit at Portland. He was assisted in his espionage by Ethel Elizabeth Gee who worked as a clerical officer in the Underwater

Detection Establishment from 1950. Houghton lived in Weymouth and Ethel Gee was a resident of Portland.

Houghton was born in Lincoln in 1906. He joined the Royal Navy in 1922 for a 22 year term, but in fact remained in the service until 1945. Before the outbreak of war he served on the China Station and in 1939 was in South Africa. During the war he had a commendable record that included sailing in the Malta and Arctic convoys. On leaving the navy he got a job as a clerk in the civil service at Portsmouth. In 1951 he was sent to the British Embassy in Warsaw, responsible to the naval attaché there. He remained abroad until October 1952, when he returned to England, starting work at Portland in the following month. He had married in 1939 and had one daughter.

Ethel Gee, though born in Hampshire, came to work on Portland at the age of 15 in a confectionery shop owned by her uncle. Apart from a period during the war when she worked at an aircraft component factory near Hamble, she was continuously employed in Portland or Weymouth. In 1950 she became a clerical officer with the Underwater Detection Establishment and met Houghton for the first time in 1952. Their relationship developed into a love affair.

From 1957 onwards, it seemed that Houghton frequently met Gordon Lonsdale in London. Test pamphlets and reports of research, obtained by Ethel Gee and passed to Houghton, were brought out of the naval base by Houghton in his car, often on a Friday. MI5, when they became aware of Houghton's activities, observed meetings between him and Lonsdale between July 1960 and January 1961. At New Year 1961, Lonsdale made one of his rare visits to Dorset. Tests of an improved anti-submarine device were to be made at Portland and the Russians wanted to know where and when. The police closed on the two Portland spies on 7 January 1961 when they were both arrested in London.

Following the trial and sentence of 15 years each to Houghton and Gee, Lord Carrington, First Lord of the Admiralty, set up a special inquiry into security weakness at the base.

The Admiralty Research Establishment acoustic calibration vessel CRYSTAL at her mooring close to the Outer Breakwater.

Cod Wars & The Falklands

The frigate HMS LINCOLN exercising off Portland. The view shows the wooden reinforcement of her bows to enable her to combat Icelandic gunboats.

HMS OSPREY

Ships of the Western Fleet assembled in Weymouth Bay in July 1969 before sailing on to Torbay for royal review and the presentation by the Queen of a new colour to the Fleet. The Commander-in-Chief, Western Fleet, Admiral Sir John Bush KCB DSC flew his flag in the aircraft carrier *Eagle*, and his ships included the nuclear submarines

Valiant and *Warspite*, the cruiser *Blake*, three destroyers, eleven frigates, six patrol submarines, three Royal Fleet Auxiliary vessels, *Abdiel* and four minesweepers, and three survey vessels.

During the disputes over fishing rights with Iceland, the so-called 'Cod Wars', frigates working up at Portland were, on occasion, placed at readiness to sail to reinforce ships already on station to support the British trawlers. Following the bumping and barging that took place between the thin hulled frigates and Icelandic gunboats strengthened against ice, the *Lincoln* and *Jaguar* were fitted with heavy timber protection to bow and stern. But this measure was never put to the test in northern waters.

The greatest emergency since the end of the Second World War occurred with the Falklands campaign of 1982.

The Argentine invasion of the Falkland Islands took place on 2 April and the British cabinet at once approved the dispatch of a task force to the South Atlantic. The first ships, including the carriers *Hermes* and *Invincible* sailed from Portsmouth on 5 April. It was immediately necessary to support and supply this force with warships from reserve

and requisitioned merchant vessels. Portland naval base played its full part in these preparations. One of the first ships to head south, the ocean going tug *Typhoon* actually sailed from Portland on Sunday 4 April, only two days after the invasion. The assault ship *Intrepid* was stored, prepared for sea and sent to Portland for operational trials and work up. With her pennant number painted out she sailed on 26 April. Three days later the patrol vessel *Leeds Castle* sailed from Portsmouth in the morning, carried out flying exercises and paused at Portland before sailing for Ascension Island in the afternoon.

The RFA *Bayleaf, Brambleleaf* and *Plumleaf* all visited Portland before sailing south. *Bayleaf* was still in the builder's hands when the crisis began, *Plumleaf* was at Gibraltar, but returned to England and spent a day at Portland before setting sail on 19 April in

company with the frigates *Ardent* and *Argonaut* and RFA *Regent*.

The Townsend Thorenson *Europic Ferry* was requisitioned on 19 April. After loading with equipment for the 2nd Parachute Brigade, vehicles and three 'Scout' helicopters, she arrived at Portland for trials three days later. On the voyage from Southampton to Portland she carried out a refuelling exercise at sea (RAS). With her trials complete she sailed for the South Atlantic on Sunday 25 April to rendezvous off Plymouth with the ill-fated *Atlantic Conveyor*. Five trawlers were requisitioned and commissioned as the 11th Mine Counter Measures Squadron, the ships becoming HMS *Cordella*, *Junella*, *Northella*, *Farnella* and *Pict*. They underwent modification at Rosyth, but before sailing for the Falkland Islands, they tested their minesweeping gear at Portland. Of the other requisitioned ships, the BP tanker *British Esk* was the first to reach Portland. Arriving on 7 April she was loaded with aviation fuel, diesel oil and ships' fuel oil and at the same time equipped for refuelling at sea. Four days later she sailed south.

Throughout the period of the emergency, the naval base was at its busiest with warships preparing to support or replace ships already in the South Atlantic. The normal work up routine, vigorously applied by FOST, was concentrated to enable ships to be ready for active service as soon as possible. At the same time the resources of the Admiralty Underwater Weapons Establishment were used in response to operational and material problems arising from Argentinian activities.

All the major warships lost in the Falklands campaign had at some time exercised in Portland waters. HMS *Sheffield, Coventry, Ardent* and *Antelope* had worked up there under the supervision of the Flag Officer Sea Training. A number of returning ships, their paintwork less than immaculate from the rigours of the South Atlantic, called at the base on the way to their home ports. Pennant numbers were painted out, and the Type 42 destroyers wore a vertical black stripe from funnel to waterline to distinguish them from their Argentinian counterparts. Ships preparing for their spells of duty at the Falkland Islands continue to be seen exercising off the Dorset coast as they prepare for their commission—"down south".

AND THE ROYAL FLEET AUXILIARY TOO. . . .

Over the years the RFA have worked up at Portland alongside warships. With fewer and fewer bases overseas these days their role becomes even more important. Modern fast ships have replaced old work horses like RFA FORT DUSQUENE seen here . . .

Portland 1987. A fine shot showing the reclaimed area forming the hardstanding for helicopters and the new accomodation buildings to the rear.

Despite past rumours of closure, the naval base at Portland is now intensely active, maintaining the long association between the Royal Navy and the communities of Weymouth and Portland. The size and composition of the fleet has changed dramatically over the years. Where once the battle squadrons lay at their moorings, surrounded by cruisers and smaller ships, there are now perhaps two or three support and replenishment ships of the Royal Fleet Auxiliary Service. The destroyer pens have gone, but in their place alongside Q Pier can be seen the modern frigates and destroyers of the NATO navies. Instead of the depot ships *Maidstone* or *Titania* and *Alecto* and their broods of submarines, a solitary NATO submarine glides in and out of harbour to exercise with surface ships. Occasionally a British or United States nuclear submarine will suddenly appear, only to depart in its own mysterious way after a brief visit. In-stead of the great fleet aircraft carriers, the new smaller *Invincible, Illustrious* and *Ark Royal* have all exercised recently off Portland and have on occasion come alongside the Coaling Pier. Not that there is any coal there for the pier has now been extended and built over. Apart from the grey warships, including

mine countermeasures ships and patrol vessels, the white survey ships with their buff funnels also work up at the base, and the distinctive red hulled ice patrol ship *Endurance* pays regular visits before her long voyages to Antarctic waters.

Experimental work at Portland continues. Research and development is carried out at the three Admiralty Research Establishments, one at Southwell close to Portland Bill, one in the Naval Base and the third at Bincleaves at the northern end of the harbour. Close to the southern breakwater, the flat bottomed trials vessel *Crystal* is anchored. She is fitted with instruments and lifting gear for acoustic research. Trials tenders, with their black hulls and brown upperworks, carry out sea trials. Royal Maritime Auxiliary Service vessels, including the *Whitehead* and *Auricula*, may be seen at Portland while testing equipment for detecting, tracking and destroying underwater targets.

Above and around the harbour, Royal Navy helicopters engage in operational training from the Royal Naval Air Station. Four squadrons normally operate from the base.

702 Squadron is equipped with the Lynx helicopter and training is provided for both

pilots and observers in the operational use of the aircraft and its equipment. The squadron also trains maintenance personnel. 772 Squadron supports the work up programmes of ships operating from Portland under the Flag Officer Sea Training (FOST). Equipped with Wessex V helicopters, the squadron transfers equipment, stores and personnel between the ships and from ship to shore. The squadron is also responsible for Search and Rescue missions from Portland. 815 Squadron moved to Portland from Yeovilton on 19 July 1982 and operates ships' flights of Lynx helicopters. Aircrew are posted to this squadron when their training is completed and detached to frigates and destroyers on operational service. The squadron also assesses new equipment for the Lynx and develops new tactics.

829 Squadron is at present responsible for all the remaining Wasp helicopters in service with the Royal Navy, though this machine is now being phased out and will be replaced by the Lynx. Aircraft of the squadron are deployed in frigates and survey vessels, including the Antarctic survey vessel *Endurance*. All these Portland based helicopters are constantly hovering, practising manoeuvres, transporting supplies and exercising with the ships at sea.

Finally, the long association between the Royal Family, the Royal Navy and Portland continues. In recent years, visits to the base have been frequent as well as to ships working up. HRH Prince Charles, as a serving officer, came to Portland in 1972 as a Sub Lieutenant aboard the destroyer *Norfolk*. Four years later he brought his command, the minehunter *Bronington* into Portland. His uncle, Earl Mountbatten, visited him on board. More recently HRH Prince Andrew has seen helicopter squadron service at Portland, both at the base itself and in a detached flight aboard the frigate HMS *Brazen*. As he continues to follow a career in the Royal Navy, the Prince and his wife, as the Duke and Duchess of York, are likely to continue the association well into the future.

HMS OSPREY

A salute to Portland? HMS SCYLLA fires a fun salute on completion of yet another 'work up'.

CONCLUSION

When the first breakwater was begun, it was unlikely that the extent of the Royal Navy's association with Portland and Weymouth could have been foreseen. The natural protection offered by the 'isle' of Portland and by Chesil Beach meant that the area would always be used as a harbour of refuge by ships that might otherwise be exposed to the Channel gales. The grand sweep of Weymouth Bay and the lee of Portland also made a suitable place for ships to assemble. Naval squadrons, prepared for particular service, whether intended for the North Sea, the Baltic or the Mediterranean, could conveniently assemble there to await orders. The Channel Fleet, if at Portland, was strategically placed to counter any aggressive moves by the French, especially from Cherbourg. As facilities were extended at the base, and particularly after the additional breakwaters were built, then Portland became a protected anchorage with all the facilities of a naval base apart from those of a major dockyard. Since the turn of the century there have been few, if any, major warships that have not spent at least a short period at Portland, while a great many minor vessels have also spent time there.

With a major fleet frequently at Portland, most naval personnel served at, or at least visited the 'island' during their naval careers. Future officers received early sail training in the brigs at Portland and many boy seamen spent their first days afloat aboard the *Boscawen* or the supporting training vessels attached to her. Officers and men came to Portland in the Channel, Atlantic or Home Fleets, serving in the battle squadrons, the cruisers, in the destroyer and submarine flotillas, exercising, working up or perhaps assembling for a fleet review by the Sovereign. During the 1939-45 war, the presence of HMS *Bee* at Weymouth brought many coastal forces personnel to the area, while combined operations and the build up to Operation Neptune added to the number of men acquainted with the harbours. Men from Commonwealth and Allied nations served at Portland as did women of the Women's Royal Naval Service. Among the many famous admirals of the Royal Navy in the last 150 years, Beatty, Beresford, Cowan, Cunningham, Fisher, Fraser, Jellicoe, Keyes, Mountbatten and Vian have all recorded occasions when they were at Portland.

Portland may not have been the most popular base at which to serve. It has not offered the same scale of social opportunities as the dockyards of Portsmouth, Plymouth and Chatham. Nearby Weymouth, a small town, is separated from Portland by the causeway of Chesil Beach. To some the island may have seemed bleak, with its massive hump dominating the anchorage, and the entrance to the Verne prison standing boldly near the top. The many stone buildings and the rocky outcrops may not have seemed inviting. Nevertheless both Portland and Weymouth have many serving and retired naval service men and women as residents. The island, the town, the rural hinterland of Dorset and the impressive and varied coastline from the Purbeck hills to West Bay combine to give a home environment that they would not change for the world.

SELECTED BIBLIOGRAPHY

Acutt, D G F
Bateson, C

Bennett, G
Bettey, J H
Brassey's Naval Annual
Brice, M
Buxton, Dr I
Capa, R
Churchill Sir W S
Churchill Sir W S
Colledge, J J
Collier, B
Corbett Sir J S &
Newbolt Sir H
Critchley, M
Cruikshank, C
Cunningham, Admiral of the Fleet
Sir A B
Dickens, Capt P
Dittmar, F J &
Colledge, J J
Everitt, D
Fell, Capt W R
Grant, R M
Gray, E
Hackmann, W
Harrison, G A
HMSO
HMSO

HMSO

Hocking, C
Holman, G
Holman, G
Hurd, A
James, Adm Sir W
Jane's Fighting Ships
Lambert, A
Laird Clowes, Sir W
Lott, A S
Mackay, R F
Manning, Capt T D &
Walker, C F
March, E J
Marder, A
Marder, A
Mariner's Mirror, The
Mayo, L
Morison, S E

Morris, S
Naval Review
Navy Lists
Neureuther, K &
Bergen, C
Parkes, O
Plumridge, J H
Ramsey, W G
Ritchie, C
Rohwer, J
Rohwer, J &
Mummelchen, G
Roskill, S W
Roskill, S W
Ryan, C
Scott, Lt Cdr P
Taylor, Lt Cdr J E
Villar, Capt R
Wettern, D
Willoughby, M F

Brigade in Action
Convict Ships

Charlie B
The Island & Royal Manor of Portland

The Tribals
Big Gun Monitors
Images of War
World Crisis 1911-1918
The Second World War (6 vols)
Ships of the Royal Navy
The Defence of the United Kingdom

Naval Operations
Falklands Task Force Pt 1, 2
The German Occupation of the Channel Islands

A Sailor's Odyssey
Night Action

British Warships 1914-1919
The K Boats
The Sea Surrenders
U Boats Destroyed
The Devil's Device
Seek and Strike
Cross Channel Attack
British Vessels Lost at Sea 1914-1918
British Merchant Vessels Lost or Damaged by Enemy Action during the
Second World War
Ships of the Royal Navy:
Statement of Losses during the Second World War
Dictionary of Disasters at Sea, 1824—1962
The Little Ships
Stand by to Beach
The Merchant Navy
The Portsmouth Letters

Battleships in Transition
The Royal Navy (7 vols)
Most Dangerous Sea
Fisher of Kilverstone

British Warship Names
British Destroyers
The Anatomy of British Sea Power
From Dreadnought to Scapa Flow

On Beachhead & Battlefront
United States Navy In World War Two: Vol XI, The Invasion of France
and Germany
Portland, an illustrated History

U Boat Stories
British Battleships
Hospital Ships & Ambulance Trains
The War in the Channel Islands
Q Ships
Axis Submarine Successes

Chronology of the War at Sea 1939—1945
The War at Sea (4 vols)
Naval Policy between the Wars (2 vols)
The Longest Day
The Battle of the Narrow Seas
The Last Passage
Merchant Ships at War
The Decline of British Sea Power
US Coastguards in World War 2

Sherrenn, D
Brown, Son &
Ferguson 1959
P Dawnay 1968
Univ. Bristol 1970

Ian Allan 1971
World Ship Soc. 1978
Hamlyn 1964
Macmillan 1943
Cassell 1948—1954
David & Charles 1969
HMSO 1957

Longmans 1920—1931
Maritime Books 1982
O U P 1975

Hutchinson 1951
Peter Davies 1974

Ian Allan 1972
Harrap 1963
Cassell 1960
Putnam 1964
Seeley, Service 1975
HMSO 1984
US Army 1951
Patrick Stephens 1977

HMSO 1947

HMSO 1947
Lloyds 1969
Hodder & Stoughton 1943
Hodder & Stoughton 1944
Murray 1921
Macmillan 1946

Conway 1984
Sampson, Low 1897
USNI 1959
Oxford 1973

Putnam 1959
Seeley, Service 1966
Cassell 1972
Oxford 1961—1970

US Army 1968

Oxford 1957
Dovecote Press 1985

Constable 1931
Seeley, Service 1966
Seeley, Service 1975
After the Battle 1981
Dalton 1985
Patrick Stephens 1983

Ian Allan 1972
HMSO 1954—1961
Collins 1968
Simon & Schuster 1959
Country Life 1946
Allen & Unwin 1946
Conway & Lloyds 1984
Jane's 1982
USNI 1957

GLOSSARY

ASDIC	Acronym used for British Anti-Submarine detection apparatus. Sometimes thought to have derived from Anti-submarine Detection Investigation Committee, though the existence of this committee is doubtful.
BRIG	usually a two masted vessel, square rigged on both masts.
CABLE	a unit of measurement at sea, 100 fathoms or 200 yards.
CONVOY	designations of convoys in the 1939—1945 war:

CE	Channel convoyeastbound.
CW	Channel convoy westbound.
OA	Southend, outward to America.
PW	Portsmouth to the Bristol Channel.
WP	Bristol Channel to Portsmouth.
TBC	UK coastal convoys supporting the invasion of France, 1944.

DOLPHIN	large wooden pile, serving in this case as a marker.
E BOAT	British name for German Motor Torpedo Boats. The German name was Schnellboote, hence S 65 etc.
FLOTILLA	a squadron of small ships.
FOIC	Flag Officer in Charge.
FOST	Flag Officer Sea Training.
GIG	a light narrow boat with single banked oars. Sometimes two short masts could be stepped for lug-sails.
HARD	a concrete ramp for loading vehicles, including tanks, into landing craft.
HSL	High Speed Launch, usually an RAF rescue launch.
HYDROPHONE	an instrument to receive sound transmitted through water.
IRONCLAD	a warship built of iron, or with a wooden hull protected by iron plates.
LCI(L)	Landing Craft Infantry (Large).
LCT	Landing Craft Tank.
LST	Landing Ship Tank.
MASB	Motor Anti-Submarine Boat.
MGB	Motor Gun Boat.
ML	Motor Launch.
MMS	Motor Minesweeper.
MTB	Motor Torpedo Boat.
MULBERRY	artificial harbour designed and built to be assembled off the Normandy coast in order to supply the Allied invasion forces, 1944.
OPERATION NEPTUNE	the assault phase of the Allied invasion of France.
OPERATION OVERLORD	the Allied invasion of France in June 1944.
PARAVANE	a form of wire cutter streamed from each bow of a ship. It was intended to cut free a moored mine pushed aside by the ship's bow wave.
PHOENIX	prefabricated steel and concrete caissons, part of the MULBERRY harbour.
'Q' SHIP	a small merchant ship, steam or sail, with concealed armament, intended to lure U boats within range.
RAS	Replishment at sea.
RDF	Radio Direction Finding, later developed into Radio Detection and Ranging (RADAR).
RFA	Royal Fleet Auxiliary.
RMAS	Royal Maritime Auxiliary Service.
SGB	Steam Gun Boat.
THREE DECKER	a sail warship with three gun decks.
VTOL	Vertical Take Off and Landing aircraft, e.g. the Sea Harrier.

INDEX

INDEX OF SHIPS

WARSHIPS AND AUXILIARIES